James Emory

M000267252

7-11-15

Adventures of a mid-America street urchin

By James Emory Thompson

(Written for the 55th year reunion of the
MASH Class of 1959 on June 20, 2014)

(Cover photo: The urchin at age 10 at
Cook Forest; no shirt and broken glasses.)

ISBN: 978-0986275913
Erie, Pennsylvania 2014

Table of contents

Webster's New World College Dictionary describes a street urchin as: "... a small child, esp. a boy who is poor, ragged, etc., and often mischievous or undisciplined."

The city is so quiet in the middle of the night. The only movement down Chestnut Street is the silent changing of the traffic signals from green to yellow to red and back again. No cars await them. The storefronts are dark and desolate – like in a sci-fi movie after the monster has struck and gone. The only other illumination is from the street lights, casting a dim glow across the landscape of downtown Meadville.

We leave the *Tribune* in my faded-gray 1949 Pontiac slant-back sedan and make our way around the silent city, dropping off bundles of newspapers to be opened in a few hours by paper boys, businesses and offices.

That was part of our routine in 1958 and 1959. Art, my younger brother, and I did these rounds after our shift in the mail room, helping with the press run and processing the 15,000 newspapers for the various forms of delivery. *The Meadville Tribune* – the *Tribune Republican* in more partisan times – was published six days a week. Our payroll slip said the shift started at 2 a.m. and ended at 5 a.m. – no matter how long it took. Pay was $1 an hour, then the federal minimum wage, or $18 a week. Take-home pay was $13 and the Texas Lunch down on Water Street would cash our fresh paychecks if we made a purchase, usually a cream-filled doughnut and a glass of milk for each of us.

At the end of our bundle route, I would take

Art home and go on to clean two restaurants, The Lamplighter Room and Johnnie's Drive-In. I had to hustle in order to make it to school by 8 a.m.

It occurred to me many times that I was driving past the silent, darkened homes of my friends and classmates – all sound asleep and assured of a hot breakfast before they headed off to Meadville Area Senior High School (MASH) in the morning.

Mine was a different Meadville. I had the same hopes and aspirations as my peers, but little in the way of family security and the normal American middle-class lifestyle so many seemed to have.

I fit the description of a street urchin from age 10 in 1951 until I took a sabbatical from Allegheny College in 1961 to enlist for three years in the U.S. Army, where you were certain to shape up quickly.

Don't feel sorry for me. I realized then and know now that many of my classmates at MASH had it pretty tough, too. Some had lost fathers in World War II. Some lived in poverty worse than ours. I know of at least one classmate who did not have indoor plumbing. His father was raising four children as a single parent on the old family farm. Others my age had disabilities and family tragedies – of which we often knew little or nothing. No, I wasn't the only one who had a rough road.

But we were kids and took life as it came. Few of my fellow street urchins felt deprived. We didn't know what we didn't have until we got older. Almost all of us had great expectations about the future and looked forward to the choices we would be making in a few years. The American middle class was beginning to blossom. Ours was truly a land of opportunity.

My story is different than many of my fellow urchins in that I didn't start out in poverty. My father, Donald C. Thompson (1891-1943), was a lawyer in Meadville. He had brown hair and brown eyes and was well over 6 feet tall. Some might have thought him handsome. He was modest in manner, though, and let his intellect speak for itself. Donald was a World War I veteran, head of Civil Defense for Crawford County, was in charge of the Meadville Armory as a captain in the Army National Guard, was a past commander of the local American Legion post, was a long-time Sunday School teacher at Stone United Methodist Church, and was a 32nd degree Mason. He and my mother had five children in seven years between 1936 and 1942. Then, like a curse, the ravages of diabetes forced him into semi-retirement early in 1943 and led to his death that May. The five of us ranged in age from six years to seven months.

Helen, the eldest, was rather small for her age with dark hair and a no-nonsense attitude about most things. She was exposed to my father's music and aspired to be an opera singer. She always has been religious and in adulthood spent four years as a Methodist missionary librarian in Argentina. She now is a church secretary in Asheville, N.C., and has written several hymns. She has no plans to retire, even as she approaches age 80.

Miriam was a genuine tomboy who took after my mother in her Welsh farm girl appearance and demeanor. Fairly large and strong, Miriam could hold her own with most of the boys who might pick on her three younger brothers. She died in 2003, having struggled for years with the ravages of diabetes.

Don, fair-haired, blue-eyed and very athletic, would not need much support. He got into the Charles Atlas body-building program before he was 12 and still works out daily at age 75. He was destined to be a Marine, a coach and a teacher. He has excelled at all three. Don also learned to play guitar, to sing, and has written a few country music songs. And he has served as a missionary pilot and has been involved in extensive religious study. He is two years older than I.

Cook Forest picnic with 1942 Plymouth, c. 1951.
From left: Don, 12; Art, 9; Helen, 14 (standing); cousin
Eleanor Parker; the urchin, 10; Momsy, 37; and Miriam, 13.

Art, who is 16 months my junior, was fair-haired and thin as a youth, and more scholarly than athletic. After three years as a linguist in the U.S. Army Security Agency, he joined the National Security Agency, graduated from the University of Maryland with high honors, and had a 35-year NSA career as an intelligence officer. It was highlighted by his graduation "with distinction" from the U.S. Naval War College in 1995. In retirement, Art has worked tirelessly as a volunteer on behalf of North Carolina residents with mental and physical disabilities. As I write this book, he is serving as president of the Mental Retardation Association of North Carolina.

I was the dark horse – large for my age with brown hair, brown eyes, and full of adventure, and occasional misadventure. My desire to understand things around me and to experience life led to a 36-year career in journalism, from 1965 to 1968 with the *Tribune* and then the *Erie Daily Times* and *Sunday Times-News* until my retirement in 2001.

Of the boys, Don has always been the patriot-warrior; Art, the pragmatic, serious scholar; and me, the romantic explorer with an interest in just about everything. Throughout childhood, I was attached at the hip with one or the other a lot of the time. But we had very different characters, as did our sisters when compared with each other. And I was apt to go out on my own more than my siblings.

Great Expectations

Meadville was the quintessential mid-America small city. The zipper, originally the hookless fastener, had been invented in our town in the late 1800s. By the 1950s Talon Inc. had nine plants, about half of them in Meadville, and what seemed to be a secure future as the world's premier manufacturer of zippers. Alas, along came plastic ones from Japan that eventually worked without snagging or breaking apart. The plastic zippers kept getting better and better until metal ones were all but obsolete. Talon is now a piece of history, one of the first American victims of the global economy. Some say its demise involved an early episode of industrial espionage. Tom Clark, a high school classmate, told me recently that Talon had developed a plastic zipper at the time World War II began and was ready to mass-produce it. During the war, however, Talon diverted its facilities to manufacturing machine gun ammunition. A few years after the war, Talon hosted a Japanese business delegation to show its new zipper production facilities as a gesture of good will. The story goes that the visitors took no notes, but plenty of photographs of Talon's machines to make plastic zippers. It wasn't too long afterward that the U.S. market began to see the Japanese plastic zippers and the slide downward began. I don't know if the story is true. But the speed at which Japan competed with American products surprised everyone.

The American Viscose plant (Avisco) made rayon and other synthetic fibers. It, too, seemed to have a secure future. But it, too, is gone. Phoenix Iron, later Sunbeam Equipment Corp., made furnaces. Meadville Malleable Iron was prosperous, as was its Kerrtown neighbor, Dad's Dog Food. American Brake Shoe manufactured train parts in a large plant out on Route 19. We had railroad repair yards and a host of small tool shops, spawned by the Talon tool room, which produced some of the best machinists in the world. The railroad businesses are now gone, too. The community, like many others across the country, slowly lost large pieces of its manufacturing base.

Meadville is the county seat of Crawford County and is surrounded by a robust farming community. On college hill stands Allegheny which can boast to be the oldest liberal arts college west of the Alleghenies under its original name. Meadville had two hospitals – today they are combined – and a vibrant business community. Its location, 500 miles from New York City and 500 miles from Chicago, made it an important railroad town prior to the era of interstate highways. In the late 19th Century, a large hotel stood adjacent to the train station to house passengers who wanted a break from travel. Pullman cars on trains came later. The station itself stood at the west end of Chestnut Street. It was red brick, two-stories high with prominent gables. It was what a movie maker would use to show a classic Civil War era depot. The tree-lined streets in town passed many beautiful homes; some old and stately, some modern and extravagant. It was a great place to grow up. Many people did not bother to lock their doors. Serious crimes rarely occurred. Many of the residential streets were paved with red brick. Most are still in use today, but the art of maintaining the brick surface seems to have been lost. Some of them now are like washboards.

I started life in a very large house out on Alden Street Extension, east of the city. We had a nanny, two stairways to run up and down, a large library and a big yard. Neighbor Henry Albaugh had a horse, which gave us great delight. When I was age three in 1944, my widowed mother moved us to a large house at 787 North Main Street, halfway between North and Randolph streets. Her wish was to get us close to First District School, the public library, Meadville High School and downtown. All essentials should be within walking distance.

My father had been a prominent lawyer, but not a wealthy one. His two living sisters, however, were involved in a family real estate business and, we were told, owned about 20 rental properties in Meadville and Titusville. The Thompson children were five of the six likely heirs for the two aunts. My mother thought we would be pretty well off. After my father's death, she invested in two rental houses with life insurance money, so a source of income was assured. Two of my mother's teen-age nieces were available to help out with child care, and a network of family friends and supporters was in place. The prospects were bright enough that she turned down an invitation from the Meadville Masonic Lodge to send us all to the Masonic Home at Elizabethtown, Lancaster County. They offered her a job on campus and family accommodations. I argued with her a few years later that she should have jumped at the offer.

**Momsy: eternal optimist
in a hard-luck life.**

Despite our occasional differences on family matters, I loved and respected my mother. In fact, I am dedicating this book to her, Laura Roberts Thompson Smith (1914-1983); and to my sister, Miriam Thompson Barkley. Miriam was three years older than I, but in the early years functioned as a second mother. It was Miriam who would get up early each morning to make the large pot of cocoa and a big pan of oatmeal, or perhaps a tray or two of cinnamon toast; who would iron our jeans as we waited to run off to school; and who broke the gender barrier in Meadville paper carriers by holding a series of *Erie Daily Times* routes until she was old enough to go to work at Johnnie's Drive-In, all to earn money for the family. Always, though, she kept an eye on college and a future that led her to a career she was made for – a caregiver at Polk Center, a residential facility for the developmentally disabled near Franklin in Venango County.

From this point on, I will call my mother Momsy. It was an affectionate nickname I gave her in my teen years after seeing the movie, "Compulsion." One of the youthful protagonists in the Leopold-Loeb murder case, the subject of the film, called his mother that and it seemed cool to me, even though the guys were not.

I am blessed or cursed, as you will, with a better than average memory. I have a good early recollection of the summer band concerts on Diamond Park. My father's two sisters owned the large, gray house at 911 Diamond. It still stands directly south of the Crawford County Courthouse, across East Cherry Street. Today, a state historical marker stands in front of the large, stately house. The blue and yellow marker is not for the Thompsons, however, but for former Pennsylvania Gov. Raymond P. Shafer, who later owned the house, and whose first law office was in the building next door. As tots, we would sit on the large pillared porch and watch the musicians play on the temporary band shell in the park. It was near the spot where a permanent shell stands now.

**Former family residence at 911 Diamond Park;
Crawford County courthouse is at left.**

Another early memory is of a Saturday
morning outside the red brick Market House in
downtown Meadville. Market days were a
community event. Momsy would take all five of us
to shop for vegetables, meats and goodies at the
booths that filled the market house building and the
area surrounding it. There was always a big crowd.
Somehow that day I became separated from the
family. I must have been only three or four years
old because I remember being placed on the
shoulders of a huge policeman, who took me up on
the first-story porch of the adjacent Kepler Hotel.
When I quit crying, he told me to look out in the
crowd and find my family. Eventually I did. He
carried me to them.

My favorite policeman back in my early
youth, however, was Officer Ed Rose. "Rosie" rode
a bright-red Indian motorcycle. He was the closest
thing I had seen to a live cowboy, whipping on the
siren to round up the speeders and those who dared

14

run red lights in our town. And no parade could be held without Rosie in the lead.

One of my jobs during World War II was to crush tin cans out by the curb on North Main Street to be collected for the war production effort. It was America's first mass attempt at recycling. Gasoline was rationed during the war and car owners were issued coupons. I can recall driving clear over to Kerrtown to gas up at Harry's service station. I believe Harry was a friend of my father's and gave Momsy a little extra – enough for her to take us on an occasional excursion to Cook Forest State Park. That trip, about 60 miles each way, was the only pleasure driving we did.

It was a big thing then to even own a car. Many families did not. I know of no Meadville family in my early years that had more than one car, except perhaps Dr. Harry Winslow, a prominent physician and the owner of our local radio station.

Another keen memory is of a late-night visit to a Cornplanter Indian tribal dance in the area near the Pennsylvania-New York border where the Allegheny Reservoir is now. We wore our Cub Scout shirts and caps and sat around a large outdoor fire on a very dark night. A ceremony began and Don and I were called to the fire and followed a ritual in which we were made blood brothers of the tribe. Though I don't believe any blood was exchanged. I was no more than age eight. Art was too young for the ritual.

It was explained to us that we received this honor because our father had done legal work, pro bono I believe, for the Cornplanters and others in the Seneca Nation. The Senecas are part of the Iroquois Confederacy, also known as the League of Six Nations. I never knew much about my father's

15

work with the League. I found a letter in his log book from a high-ranking official of the League, which is headquartered near Syracuse, N.Y. Written in 1939, the letter wished my father well in his illness and thanked him for his efforts on behalf of the League. Review of a contract of some kind was discussed. The Cornplanters have been fighting for land rights along the Pennsylvania-New York border for a long time. Perhaps his work pertained to that. Many Cornplanters were displaced in the 1960s by U.S. government land acquisition for the Allegheny Reservoir. Bitterness still exists today.

I also recall from childhood memory the day that Momsy danced. I never saw her dance before or after. It was on May 8, 1945. I came down the stairway to see her in the living room, dancing in circles like a whirling dervish. She saw me and shouted, "Jimmy, the Germans have surrendered!" It was Victory in Europe Day, or VE Day, as it is called now. VJ Day was to follow in August that year when the Japanese surrendered. The war was over.

By 1949, the two aunts, Anna Bunce and Edith Thompson, had died and Momsy was fighting in the courts for her children's inheritance. But the real estate did not come to us. We ended up with only a small trust fund that was not readily available. Also dying about then was our neighbor, William Emory Hyskell, M.D., who had been my father's best friend and our assurance of adequate health care. Few people had health insurance in those days. You paid at the office when you received the services. If you had nothing to pay with, you were in a tough position. Dr. Hyskell had treated us as if we were his own children.

So Momsy already had been dealt two blows in her plan to raise her five children in Meadville. The third blow was the gradual impact of post-war inflation. My father had left us a 1942 – yes a 1942 – Plymouth four-door sedan. He had been able to obtain that maroon beauty prior to his illness because of his Civil Defense role. Detroit quit making new cars for civilians in late 1941, right after Pearl Harbor. We had one of only a few 1942 models in town. Momsy, who had learned to drive shortly after my father's death, ordered a new Plymouth from Weber Motors in 1947 or 1948. Art and I went down to see the sleek gray sedan after it arrived at the garage on North Street. The sticker price jumped by $200 before Momsy could close the deal – I believe from about $800 to $1,000. She couldn't afford it. We drove our 1942 "Lizzie" until it died in 1952. By the end of the 1940s, Momsy was all but broke. She began working whatever jobs she could find – sometimes three at once. It is no surprise that she lost full control of her five young children.

Donald C. Thompson:
scholar, lawyer, soldier.

Huck Finn, Tom Sawyer rescued

A harbinger of the loose cannon I was to become occurred when I was in third grade at First District School. Rodney McDonald and I got out of school on a chilly, overcast February afternoon and went to his house on Terrace Street, near the Spring Street Bridge over French Creek.

He told me he had found a raft in the large temporary pond nearby that was formed by overflow waters from French Creek. That low-lying area below Terrace Street was part of the old canal system that Meadville was establishing when the railroad came in the 1860s. The trains rendered the canals obsolete before they were of much use and the channels were soon abandoned. Between the pond and the creek were the raised railroad lines and some old railroad shops, so there was no danger of the raft floating to the creek. It seemed to be safe enough.

The raft was about four-by-six-feet and it came with one long pole. We never found out who built it. The water in the pond was pretty deep, we knew, because that is dry ground most of the year and we had played down there a lot. It would likely be over our heads if we fell in.

But boys will be boys and we set out from shore at what I would say was 4 p.m. and had a lot of fun poling the raft around the pond. After a while it got colder, some light snow began to fall, and darkness approached. No problem, we thought, it was only a few yards to shore.

You can imagine how surprised we were when the raft quit moving. Ice had formed over the whole pond, and we were stuck. Now it was dark and growing colder by the minute. Our calls for help were not heard. We decided the best thing to do was to wait until we saw headlights of cars on Terrace Street, which was up what I would estimate to be a 60-foot hill.

Few cars passed. When one did, we shouted "Help, help!" No one stopped – until about 8 p.m. A taxi driver named Lee Adams had his window down a bit to smoke and he heard our cries and stopped. We implored him to come down and help us, but he wisely went to a house and called the Meadville Fire Department. Then came the sirens and the trucks and the spotlights.

The first fireman to try to enter the water in his hip boots went right up to his waist. They pulled him out. No way was anyone going to wade in to get us.

Assistant Fire Chief Fred Carmen, who was in charge, then called out and asked if either of us was a Cub Scout. I said yes, as I was, and he asked if I knew how to tie knots. "Yes," I said.

Carmen then had his guys slide a rope out on the ice, now about half an inch thick, cautioning us not to fall overboard trying to grasp it. After a few tries, I caught the sliding rope and tied it to the raft. Then, the firemen carefully pulled the raft inch by inch through the ice.

Luckily, we were not suffering from hypothermia and were otherwise no worse for wear when they lifted us to shore. In fact, I thought the whole thing was a pretty neat, if scary, adventure.

Rodney's dad came and took him home, which was not far away. Carmen put me into the department's brand new, bright-red Studebaker chief's car and drove me home, several blocks away. I was pretty proud of myself for keeping my cool and tying the rope securely.

'Huck Finn,' 'Tom Sawyer' Are Rescued

Two 8-year-old Meadville boys last night nursed wet and freezing feet and regretted trying to play Huck Finn and Tom Sawyer in February.

Ralph McDonald of Terrace Street and James Thompson, son of Mrs. Laura R. Thompson, 787 North Main Street, yesterday afternoon built themselves a raft and paddled into the back waters of French Creek between the Erie Railroad shops and old National Bearing Metals plant.

Mr. McDonald looked vainly for his son from 5 p.m. until almost three hours later, when a neighbor reported to Central Station firemen that two boys were calling for help.

Earlier, Lee Adams, a driver for Lafayette Taxi Service, tried to wade into the freezing waist-deep water for a rescue and couldn't make it. He helped as firemen threw a coil of rope to the young sailors. The youngsters tied the rope to their craft and were towed to shore by firemen.

Taken to their homes in the shiny new red chief's car, they received a lecture from Assistant Fire Chief Fred Carman on what might have happened to them, then they got dinner, dry clothes and massages for frozen feet.

The Meadville Tribune, Feb. 16, 1950

21

Momsy did not view the whole episode with the same sense of adventure and relief – even after I told her of the thrill of riding in the new chief's car. She took me upstairs and spanked me. I couldn't understand why I was being punished. Looking back now, after my 36 years as a journalist, I wonder why the *Tribune* reporter that night did not interview Tom and Huck. It would have made a much better story than the news brief that appeared in the *Tribune* the next morning, in which only Carmen was interviewed. The clever part of the article was the headline: "Huck Finn, Tom Sawyer are rescued."

I do remember Carmen lecturing us at the scene on the danger of what we had done, and what might have happened had Adams not heard our calls for help. The next day at First District School, our teacher, Mrs. McNutt, said, "There are two boys in this classroom today who, except for luck, wouldn't be here." Would we have frozen to death? It got pretty cold that night. I think the answer is yes. I usually did not wear a hat and often went without gloves and proper boots – even when I had them.

Later, as a *Tribune* reporter, I joked with Fred Carmen about the incident. I never got a chance to thank Lee Adams. Rodney and I continued to pal around, but were restricted mostly to his house.

To others who might contemplate such an adventure, I would say, "Don't." Mother Nature has no sympathy for bad human judgment.

Too much freedom?

I would categorize myself in those early years as a mix of the molds of Tom Sawyer, Huckleberry Finn and the artful dodger from "Oliver Twist." I was always curious and seeking new adventures. I didn't worry too much about consequences. I always believed the adventure was worth the risk, within reason. My real path to freedom came at about age 10 when brother Don showed me how to slide down the corner post of the back porch roof to the ground. We could sneak out from our back bedroom window whenever we wanted. And we often did. On our return we shinnied back up to the porch roof and no one was the wiser. It was much easier going down. We had to help each other for the return part.

It was also at age 10 that I got my wheels. I had started delivering Erie newspapers in Meadville in about 1950 – too young to even apply for a more lucrative *Tribune* morning route. I began with an *Erie Dispatch* route covering the entire north end of town, with a total of 13 customers. Remember the Sanida Dairy Bar across from Allegheny's Brooks Hall at Park Avenue and Prospect Street? I would stop there on my way back down the hill on cold evenings to get a cocoa. I only earned a few cents a day. Most went for snacks. One fond memory is sitting at a booth there to warm up while the juke box played a new hit song, Patti Page's "Tennessee Waltz." It was a sad song, but her voice warmed you up. It could get very cold on that long walk. I recall one day during a blizzard when Momsy sent Miriam and our faithful junkyard dog, Laddie, to find me and help me trudge home through the deep snow.

I had one really lucrative day as a paper carrier. In the fall of 1952, a California congressman named Richard M. Nixon was running for vice president with General Dwight D. Eisenhower on the Republican Party ticket. Nixon was on a train tour of western Pennsylvania and gave his stump speech in Pittsburgh that particular morning, with the train then heading north for a noon stop at Meadville. The *Erie Daily Times*, Erie's afternoon paper, which I then delivered, picked up the text from The Associated Press and had the speech almost verbatim in the early afternoon edition. Bus Wurst, the *Times* circulation manager in Meadville, alerted me and I shot down from First District School at lunch break, grabbed all the papers I could carry, and ran the short block to the train station. A crowd had assembled to hear Nixon speak and I sold more papers than I could believe. Everyone wanted to follow along as he delivered his speech from the rear platform of the passenger train. That was a big day for a young boy and started what became a lifelong love of politics and newspapers.

Momsy had given big brother Don a used purple Schwinn bicycle for Christmas 1950. In the summer of '51, I had learned how to ride and felt I had to have a bike as soon as possible. Our backyard neighbor, Donnie Riddle, had a shiny new Firestone – green and cream – with a decorative tank between the crossbars, a chain guard, reflectors, a headlight, whitewall tires and all of the other bells and whistles.

What was I to do? I started saving paper route pennies and scarfing up old bike parts. Some I got from Joe Sivik's junk yard over in the Fifth Ward and some from a used bicycle store on Arch

Street. I traded old toys for a wheel here and a chain there. I had to rebuild the brakes – the infamous 21 discs – in the rear wheel hub. Bikes then had no gears or hand brakes. You braked by reversing the pedals, which stopped the chain and the discs then brought the rear wheel to a halt. The discs had to be placed perfectly for the mechanism to work. I labored for hours to get the hub put together right. Both of the wheels that I found had missing spokes, which were a trick to install, and both had bald or missing tires and inner tubes. Fenders were hard to find and expensive. So I went without them. I soon had a basic 26-inch bike that carried me around Meadville until I began driving at age 16. My bike had no real color scheme – maybe a combination of rust and gray, with red and white blotches. But it worked and it was fast. I could hold my own in frequent races with Don and beat almost any other kid in town. I loved that bike. Building it was quite an achievement, I thought, even if some of my friends laughed when I had to ride it in the rain with no fenders. I got pretty wet all over.

For the paper routes, you wrapped the straps of your canvas newspaper bag over the bike handlebars. You rolled the papers up at the circulation office so you could deliver a lot of them by tossing the paper onto the porch as you rode by a customer's house. It was an art to get them folded securely so they would not fly open when hurtling through the air. One time I got carried away and flung the paper onto a porch roof. Luckily, the lady was home and let me go up the stairs and out a window to fetch it. She even offered me a snack, out of kindness. For the *Erie Times* routes, I would deliver the papers during the school lunch hour.

You really had to hustle and pray the truck from Erie, 40 miles to the north, arrived on time. Lunch was usually a Twinkie and bottle of chocolate milk at one of the small grocery stores along the route. Not a very healthy diet. I later found I was one of the happiest customers when we ate at the high school cafeteria. A hot wholesome meal for lunch. Wow!

It was also at age 10 that I befriended Don Hauck, who took me to his house on Walnut Street after school. There, we smoked cigars from a stash his mother kept but did not monitor. I got sick the first few times, but then began to enjoy the tobacco taste. It wasn't his fault, but that started a smoking habit that plagued me for 46 years. I broke my three-pack-a-day cigarette habit in 1997 through hypnosis. My lungs were saved and that is probably why I am still alive to write this book.

My nicotine addiction might have been nipped in the bud if the attendant at the gas station that was located at the corner of North Street and Park Avenue had been a faster runner. I was in there one day getting a pack out of the machine when he challenged me. Kids were not allowed to buy cigarettes. I must have been about 12. I lied to him, saying they were for my mother. When he didn't believe me, I took off running along North Street. He tried, but couldn't catch me. I wish now that he had. I tried hard to avoid telling lies. But addicts will do almost anything when threatened with discovery and interdiction. I wish today's teens showed more of an understanding of the dangers of nicotine and other addictive drugs.

Poor, with dignity

Momsy never pretended we had money. She spelled it right out to us that we had to get by with what we had and should not expect to possess all of the things other children had. But she stressed that poverty was not an embarrassment if you tried your best to get out of it, and was no excuse for bad behavior. She tried her best to instill in us the basic values of honesty, morality, family loyalty, love of country, and the importance of education. You did not swear in our house and you always showed up at a reasonable hour so she could do a daily head count between her jobs. Momsy borrowed money from relatives and friends on quite a few occasions. She sometimes would take me with her on borrowing trips as I was the child who looked most like my father – and almost all of our benefactors had known my father. By the time I was 13, I asked her to quit buying me Christmas and birthday presents because it hurt me too much that the money to buy them might have been borrowed, and she would have to pay it back some day.

Younger readers might wonder why she did not just go to the bank, or use a credit card to borrow money. Credit cards did not appear in our economy until the 1960s. And at first, only men were approved. It wasn't until 1974, under the Equal Employment Opportunity Act, that banks were prohibited from denying credit cards to women because of their gender. Meadville's bankers were, as a group, very conservative and not about to issue a personal loan to a widow with five children who had no secure employment.

Meadville, like most American small cities in the mid-20th Century, had an economic class system. I would describe the classes as the wealthy few, the business and industrial management class, the urban working class, and farmers. Businessmen held the political and economic power. I'd say that in layman's economic terms they could be called benevolent paternalists. Workers were expected to show up on time, to be loyal and not rock the boat. In return, they had steady jobs and a wage high enough to raise a family, or at least get by. Women, for the most part, were expected to be homemakers. The number of women working grew dramatically during and after World War II, but was still a small percentage of the work force. Unions were few, although there was a union headquarters in a building on Chestnut Street. Few people knew what the letters, AFL-CIO stood for. Wages varied around town, but none were close to the big-paying jobs of the major cities. Car-pooling came into being out of necessity, as groups of Meadville workers would ride together 40 miles each way to Erie each day to work at the General Electric appliance plant, which is now a locomotive plant. Workers there were well-paid and had something called benefits.

When I was a reporter for the *Tribune* in the late 1960s, I was "loaned out" to the Meadville Area Industrial Commission to write a 10-year history of the organization and its efforts to bring industry to our area. During my interviews and research, I learned that Pittsburgh Plate Glass Co. was being lured to build a float-glass plant on the site of the Keystone Ordnance Works, 10 miles south of the city. The plant had operated during World War II, and then closed. The only concern of

MAIC seemed to be that PPG would disrupt the local pay scales by offering wages higher than those at the existing plants. PPG came, the plant flourished, and the local economy survived quite well.

The business and industrial leaders with whom I dealt on the history project were good men. They were well-educated and responsible citizens. They had been taught that the economic model under which we lived was what made America great, and what brought our nation triumphantly through World Wars I and II.

The biggest problem was the underlying pressure for a more even distribution of wealth, a nationwide movement that would bring about civil disruption in the America of the 1960s and greatly expand the middle class. In Meadville, though, most workers I knew were satisfied if they could afford a modest home and a new car every few years. The '60s brought no great upheaval to small-city America.

Dodging Rudy's broom

I am getting ahead of myself here. Back about 1950 when I was grown enough to wander off by myself, the North Street business district became my "domain." I would meander down the long block from North Main to Liberty streets, looking into Judd Brown's grocery store (later Doc Rice's news stand), Cargo Cleaners, Nick Zoria's grocery, Isaly's dairy store, and Hank Neely's Corner Newstand at Liberty Street. Small businesses were prosperous then. Malls did not come for another 10 years. The North Street district was lively, but much smaller than the downtown district only a few blocks away.

The first adult to call me an urchin was Rudy Thomas. He owned Rudy's Blue Star, a popular North Street watering hole in that block. Rudy spoke with an eastern-European accent, had jet-black hair, walked with a limp and always wore a large white apron. He was extremely proud of his business and his Kielbasa sandwiches. Every afternoon Rudy would sweep the sidewalk in front of the tavern. It became a pattern that when I would try to pass he would chase me with the broom and take a somewhat serious swipe at me. "Get away you urchin," he would shout. He never did hit me, though. Rudy and I became close friends 20 years later. From 1968 into 1969, I ran the *Erie Times-News* Meadville office, located on North Street just a door or two away from Rudy's. Allegheny College friends and I frequented his place. He would even walk over with a sandwich for me when he saw me typing away in my storefront office on a Saturday night deadline. I think it shows that sometimes you have to know someone over a period of time to see the good in him or her. That was true for both of us. He explained to me that he chased me away back then because he did not want kids to be seen hanging around outside his tavern.

At First District School we learned to fear the atomic bomb because the Russians had it and threatened more than once to use it. When the air raid siren went off, we were herded out of our classrooms into the main first- and second-floor hallways where we had to sit against the wall, bent over with our heads between our legs. When we got the all-clear, we were shuttled back to our classrooms. I have no idea how effective that process would have been had an atomic bomb been dropped. I doubt if it would have helped much. Many people in America built air raid shelters in their yards during the Cold War. They were stocked with provisions and offered some hope of survival. Don got into the act and had Art and I help him dig a deep foxhole in the middle of our back yard. Momsy had a fit. Don, by then, was in his John Wayne years – destined to become a Marine. He later served as a Marine lieutenant in Viet Nam and got a real taste of war. He is still very proud of his service to his country.

The fear of air attack was not new to the Cold War. During the 1930s, my father went around to area granges, churches and other meeting places, preaching the dangers of Germany and the weapons systems the Nazis were developing. Many thought the Germans would sooner than later have a plane or rocket that could strike the United States. Few people know it, but by the time we entered the war, they did. Luckily, it was never used against us. The German submarines did play havoc with Allied shipping off our Atlantic coast. Meadville was in the industrial belt stretching from Buffalo to Pittsburgh – The Ruhr Valley of America, my father called it. It would have been a logical target for any enemy attacking the United States. Authorities decided we should have air raid drills and my father was in charge of those for Meadville and the rest of Crawford County. The main part of the drill was to pull down your black window shades to darken the city should bombers fly over. Not all residents cooperated. I believe frustration over that led in part to my father's declining health and premature death.

The Cold War stayed hot for years. In ninth grade at the old Meadville High School, one of our civics class assignments was to interview a local business or government leader. I chose then-District Attorney Raymond P. Shafer. Shafer, who was a decorated World War II PT boat skipper, kindly agreed to the interview. In it, I naively asked him if he thought Crawford County was ready for an atomic attack. Shafer gave me a big fatherly smile before answering that no one could really prepare for an atomic war, not even a district attorney. I should have known right then that Ray was headed for big things.

First District School housed grades one through eight. Most of us started at age six. I had never heard of kindergarten or pre-school. The city had three other elementary schools – Second District (where my aunt, Edith Thompson, was principal for years) East End and Third District School in the Fifth Ward. In addition, North End School on North Main Street hill housed grades one through four and served the kids who lived up the hill in the upscale neighborhoods. For fifth grade, they had to join the rest of us at First District down at the bottom. Just outside the city were Kerrtown School and Neason Hill School. I believe all of the school buildings were two-story, red-brick with concrete entranceways. They must have used the same architect nationwide.

Eighth-grade class at First District School, 1955: urchin, top row, fourth from right; Miss Nancy Martin, seated, left. Photo-Graphic Arts photo.

I remember when I was invited about second grade to Linda Miller's house on Spring Street for her birthday party. I had never gone to a "formal" social event before and was so excited I could barely stand it. I think I shook the entire time I was there, then went home and bragged about it for hours to torment my siblings.

I got some early language training from my friends. In second grade at First District School, Carmella Gionti playfully swore at me in Italian. I knew the phrase, but made the mistake of

33

responding in English. Guess whose mouth Mrs. Thoma washed out with soap?

First District gave me my first taste of culture. I recited my first poem, "The Adventures of Mr. Toad," on the stage there – a frightened little ragamuffin of a boy looking out over what seemed to be a vast audience assembled in the gymnasium. The poem was inspired by "The Wind in the Willows." I remember the first few lines of my effort: *"Now my story starts in England way back in the days of old. And the hero of my story, yes, his name is Mr. Toad. When Toad was just a little chap and knee-high to a duck, he fell into a water hole and, by Jove, he got stuck."* It goes on for four or five stanzas, but I think you get the drift.

I got through the recital, but no one shined that day as did Tony Pero when he sang, "I don't want no more of Army life, Gee Mom I want to go home." Some of us thought Tony might be the next Frank Sinatra. But he turned out to be a much better basketball player than a singer.

In that small gym, teacher Ken Nelson patiently taught us the fundamentals of basketball, volleyball and gymnastics. He was perfect for the elementary schools because he was short in stature for a man and seemed more of an equal to his young charges. When a few of us at about eighth grade realized we were taller than our gym teacher, we felt like big shots.

The greatest discovery during the mid-1950s was the polio vaccine developed by Dr. Jonas Salk. Polio struck fear into the hearts of all parents. It could cripple or even kill a child and nothing could be done to stop it – until the vaccine. First, we were given shots; then booster shots; then pills; and more pills. The overkill might explain how dreaded the disease was. The vaccine worked. Polio was eradicated in our nation almost overnight.

Everyone had their favorite teachers at First District. Looking back, I believe all of them were very competent and dedicated. My favorites, though, were in the upper grades – Dorothy Buchanan in history and Nancy Martin in English. Miss Buchanan took an interest in me despite some bad behavior on my part. She "punished" me by making me stay after school and memorizing the Preamble to the U.S. Constitution and Lincoln's "Gettysburg Address." She later was one of the strongest supporters of my journalism career. Nancy Martin was a young Thiel College graduate who simply loved reading – and inspired that love in her students. Learning the art of teaching from Miss Buchanan, Miss Martin made me stay after school and memorize William Wordsworth's "Daffodils," "In Flanders Fields" by John McCrae, and Henry W. Longfellow's "Prelude to Evangeline." I should not forget science teacher John Nace, who was from Texas. He coached me through the construction of a paper-clip electric motor that actually turned over a few times when connected to a battery. A Thomas Edison I was not, but at least it sort of worked and gave me hope for better things to come.

Teachers were not paid well in those days and their pensions were meager. I never even considered teaching as a profession because of that. Miss Buchanan bolstered her pension in retirement by selling real estate; Mr. Nace, insurance. I now admire the way the teacher unions have worked for good wages and pensions over the past 60 years. People who think they are overpaid should sit in a classroom for a few days.

Doomsday walk

The worst experience a First District student could have, I was told at the very beginning, was a trip to the principal's office, where Miss Carolyn Corey ruled with an iron fist. You didn't want to go there, period.

Well, during eighth grade another boy brought a pornographic cartoon book to school. It was one of those Mutt and Jeff mini comic books. You could flip through the pages and see some crude sex going on. Sort of like the first motion-picture cameras. He had it outside at recess and guess who got caught leafing through it. The hallway never seemed so long and so dark as it was when I was paraded to the dreaded office of Miss Corey. I think she had been tipped off because she knew just what she was talking about the minute I entered the room and stood in front of her, shaking like a leaf. I probably was larger than she at the time, but she looked like a giant, staring at me with a frown on her face that would befit an executioner who loved his trade. She asked for my version of the story. I told her everything except who brought the porn to school. I wasn't really sure who it was. She believed me because she said she would not tell my mother so long as I promised to never look at porn again. I was ready to promise anything. She let me go. Whew!

When I was 12, my mother gave me a BB rifle for Christmas. Donnie Riddle had one. Brother Don got one, so I had to have one, too. She somehow came up with the money. We took the BB guns up to the ravine east of Highland Avenue for target practice in the woods. One day Donnie Riddle shot Don with one of the pellets. I believe it was accidental, but Don was very angry and Donnie took off running along a side street. I reacted as I thought any brother would. I shot Donnie Riddle twice in the back. Don says he shot him, too, but I don't remember that. Donnie had welts on his back for a few days. I did not feel good about the incident and was relieved that neither playmate was injured seriously. Must have been our old family Quaker connection in New Jersey, but I decided to give up guns for good. I was issued a rifle during part of my Army enlistment, but took no pleasure in the thought I might have to use it.

We had loose-knit gangs during those years, but no violence and no weapons. Gun laws were strictly enforced and a switch-blade knife could land you in real trouble. I had a pocket knife, which I used mostly to shave tree branches to roast hotdogs. I think our generation knew that lethal weapons were self-defeating in the hands of young people. The responsibility of gun ownership includes training, discipline, judgment and understanding. Without all of those, tragedy is likely.

The only acquaintance I had back then who had a handgun was Mike Trask. Mike was a self-described misfit. He took Don home with him after school one day and used his mother's dishes for target practice in the back yard. One day he brought his handgun to school and showed it around. He got into plenty of trouble for that, but managed to stay out of reform school.

Another time about 1956, Mike and Don decided to hitchhike to Erie on a Sunday afternoon, and invited me to tag along. We got there and roamed State Street for a while. Then we met a guy exiting a bar who offered us a ride back to Crawford

County. He had a 1951 Kaiser sedan, which we were told later had been stolen. On the way out of Erie he hit speeds close to 100 mph. I wanted out, but just ducked down in the back seat and hoped for the best. He drove west toward Ohio, then down Route 18 to Conneautville. There, he decided to pull into an old service station with free-standing gas pumps and hit one of them as he came to a sliding stop. He just shook his head and told the attendant to pump gas from the bent pump. After the fueling, he stopped to take care of some business in a mobile home park in Conneautville. Then we drove on south. When we got to Conneaut Lake, he asked us to get out as he wanted to go on south on Route 18. We did so gladly and hitched another ride the 10 miles back to Meadville. I was happy to get home alive.

The last time I saw Mike Trask was in the late 1960s. He was walking down Park Avenue with a young woman in each arm, both quite obviously pregnant. Mike was wearing his cowboy hat and cowboy boots. It was quite a sight. He told me he was working as a sheep herder out in Wyoming or Montana. Later, I learned that he was killed there when his hut burned to the ground. I never learned if the fire was accidental. With Mike, anything was possible.

Holey jeans and onions

I didn't worry too much about what I wore. Being the middle of three boys in a poor family, I usually was the hand-me-down guy. I was quite large for my age in those pre-teen years, which made me the right size for Don's discards even though he was two years older. Art was 16 months younger than I and thinner for his age. That put me third in line when it came to new boys' clothes. Like most kids our age, our outfits consisted of blue jeans and T-shirts, with sweat shirts for the fall and winter. I did all right with Don's old duds and a new shirt now and then. Shoes were another matter. All were worn out by the time we were ready for the next size. I know that among our benefactors were Manny and Millie Barkin, who ran the Factory Shoe Store on Water Street. They gave Momsy the credit she almost always needed to get back-to-school shoes for all of us. Also very helpful was the Meadville Lions Club, which provided me with new eyeglasses about as fast as I could break the pair I had; and the Kiwanis Club, which sponsored YMCA memberships for poor kids. They also sponsored the summer camp on Pymatuning Lake, which became a life-changer for me.

When I think about my jeans, I didn't know I was setting a trend that would take hold two generations later. Many that I wore had unintentional holes in the knees and pockets. Yes, I was the first holey jeans guy. Today they buy them that way.

None of the boys over age five wore shorts back then. I guess shorts were not masculine enough. The girls often wore pedal pushers, which extended below the knee, and dresses that always

39

extended below the knee. Shorts and short shorts came later.

Momsy tried to keep some sense of normalcy in our cluttered house at 787 North Main. She was always busy, even though the work never seemed to get done. I remember her canning tomatoes, peaches, beef and green beans just as she did in her childhood on the farm. Peaches were my favorite. She would load us in the car and drive to Erie County, where you could pick your own from the fruit-laden trees. We'd fill the trunk of the car with containers of peaches and head home. Momsy's challenge was to get them canned before we ate them all.

She was quite clever, too, when it came to persuading us to eat lean meals during lean times. I recall her convincing us that bread, milk and onions made a very delicious meal. I was skeptical, but the concoction filled our tummies and was pretty healthy.

I never went hungry, except maybe for a few hours now and then. Momsy always had something nourishing on the stove and, especially in the early years, had some great meals. We ate out occasionally at the Dinner Bell restaurant on Market Street. We went to Grace Methodist Church as children, and participated in the Cub Scouts at the American Legion. The Legion post also sponsored other activities, including big Christmas parties that were a highlight of the year for us. Had things become desperate, Momsy would have taken whatever measures necessary to make sure we were housed, fed and clothed. However, I did sometimes envy the kids up at the Odd Fellows Home, north of the college on North Main Street. They had three squares, an indoor gym and pool, and health care.

Then I looked at our close-knit family and said, no, this is just fine.

Fortunately, I was blessed with good health throughout those early years. I think I saw a doctor only twice, save for assembly-line sports physicals. When I was about eight and Don, 10, Momsy got a package deal from Meadville City Hospital to remove two sets of tonsils – his infected tonsils, my healthy ones. The surgery did not go well for me. I remember being in a bed at the hospital when Momsy showed up with a book titled: "The Little Red Engine That Could." It was a child's picture book about a train struggling, but finally making it to the top of a steep hill. The engine kept repeating, "I know I can; I know I can." That and ice cream brought me through.

The second doctor visit was when I was about 12 and had athlete's foot so badly that it infected the lymph glands in my groin. That was scary and I finally showed Momsy. She managed to get me to Dr. Kenneth A. Hines, classmate Ed Hines' father, who had his office in their home on Chestnut Street. He gave me medicine that worked and, as best I can remember, treated me either free or for a very small fee. Ed tells me his father often did that. We had no dental care and that became a big problem later for me. I think it was all about money. Dental care could usually wait. Some of the other children needed medical treatment from time to time. When it was serious, Momsy found a way.

Somehow, I received eye exams from Dr. Fisher on a regular basis. (I never knew him to have a first name) Either he did it for a small fee; or through the Lions Club; or simply out of goodness. My nearsightedness kept getting worse and I kept breaking eyeglasses. It was often a fuzzy world through my eyes.

Years later, Momsy told me how very badly she felt about the lack of health care we had while growing up. She considered it to be her greatest failure. Today, the government tries to ensure that all children have medical and dental care until they reach adulthood. I suffered greatly because we did not have that safety net then.

Shopping as entertainment

During those first post-war years when she still had money, Momsy loved to take us to Cleveland and Erie to shop and to catch a movie at one of the grand theaters. Euclid Avenue boasted a row of theaters in downtown Cleveland, each trying to out-glitter the others. We would shop for clothes within our means at Higbee's and the May Company. I also remember running free around Public Square in front of the huge Terminal Tower while Helen, the cultured one, attended the opera a block or two away and Momsy shopped. She would just turn the four of us loose. No sense in trying to keep us together in a crowded store. She gave us a meeting place and a time and we always showed up.

In Erie, the movie theater choices were the Warner and the Strand. The Boston Store was a favorite shopping experience because of the open escalators, from which you could see the floor below and the floor above; and the overhead network of pneumatic tube cash carriers that would zip from the sales counter to the money office at each purchase and zip back with the receipt and change. I could watch them all day. Zip. Zip.

In Meadville, our favorite stores included Wolff's Hardware, where they had the neatest toys; and the Crawford Store, where we just walked through quietly and looked at the fine array of goods we couldn't afford. We were more likely to buy clothes from the Sears catalog, or from Murphy's or Woolworth's five and ten cent stores. Many of our older friends bought their clothes at Printz's and Weldon's, but the prices at those classy shops were beyond our means.

The best Christmas present I ever received came from Wolff's in 1949. It was a bright red pump scooter. Yes, a pump scooter. You used one foot to get the scooter rolling, then stood on the platform and pumped a pedal to keep it going with both feet off the ground. I knew Momsy couldn't afford it, but I begged and begged in hope. It was a very special moment that Christmas morning when I crept down the open stairway and peered through the sliding double doors into the living room, where the large Christmas tree stood. There, with a ribbon around the handlebar, was the red scooter. I almost fainted with joy. That scooter lasted about two years before I wore it out.

For refreshment, a real treat was a Cherry Coke at Little Wirt's drug store at North Main and North streets, or Big Wirt's down on Chestnut Street. At Isaly's, you could get a wonderful ice cream bar directly from Mrs. Riddle, Donnie's mother, who managed the North Street store. The company also had a downtown store on Chestnut Street. Isaly's chipped-chopped ham is still a deli favorite in our region.

Our generation changed popular music forever. I can remember sitting at the soda fountain in early 1956 listening to that amazing voice singing "Heartbreak Hotel." After that blockbuster, Elvis Presley released a flow of hits one right after the other. We held our collective breaths for the next Elvis song. Other trend setters included Bill Haley and the Comets ushering in the new era with "Rock Around the Clock"; and Fats Domino resurrecting "Blueberry Hill" as a rock 'n' roll ballad. He helped transform pop into rock. Fading into the past were such soothing voices as those of Perry Como, Frank Sinatra and Patti Page. The big band era, too, was over; though Jimmy Dorsey revived it briefly with his 1957 hit, "So Rare." One might say the pop era ended symbolically with Dean Martin singing "Memories Are Made of This."

Groceries were purchased in the early years from the small neighborhood stores. We had Judd Brown's at North and North Main; Grippi's and Nick Zoria's on North Street; Straw's at North Main and Randolph streets; and, later, Pat and Pete's on North Main, which was our first semblance of a supermarket. Kroger's later came to North Street and the little guys began to struggle – their doom slowly but surely sealed by the emerging chain supermarkets. Momsy would walk a few of us to the store with her and we would trek home, each carrying a bag or two of groceries.

Milk was delivered to the house. Over the years we bought from Steere's Hilgendorf and Roos-Hotson dairies. The Roos-Hotson milk was pasteurized, but not homogenized, so the cream rose to the top. Nothing got me out of bed more quickly than the Roos-Hotson clatter of glass bottles on the front porch. I would pour the rich cream on my Cheerios. With a scoop of brown sugar, it was a real treat. Bananas were hard to come by. But add one to that bowl and you were in breakfast heaven. The slower siblings got the skim milk.

This was before the time of government assistance. A safety net was something they used for high-wire acts in the circus. We did get what they called surplus food from time to time. Momsy would drive us over to the side door of the Armory to get it first thing in the morning. She didn't want people to know we needed handouts. She was too proud for that. But the food really helped.

My favorite super market item was the invention called oleomargarine. It came in a sealed plastic bag – a white vegetable oil substance hydrogenated to the consistency of soft clay surrounding an orange liquid in a ball. My job was to squeeze the sealed package all over until the ball disintegrated and turned the entire package an even yellow. I was task-oriented, so Momsy gave me that job. When we got an electric wringer washing machine, I also was helpful. I was fascinated by the wringer and how it squeezed the water out of the clothes without anyone having to crank it. Occasionally a pair of jeans or a twisted towel would jam the wringer and the two rollers would pop apart. My job was to clear the jam and press the housing over the wringers until the rollers locked back into place. The wet clothes were carried out to the back yard to be hung on clothes lines. Electric and gas clothes dryers were a few years in the future for families at our income level.

My first regular domestic job was a couple of years earlier when I became the go-to guy for stoking the furnace. Our large house was heated by a coal furnace for the first few years we lived there. I loved the dark, mysterious basement because my grandfather's carpenter tools were down there, along with a couple of old kayaks and tons of other junk to explore. I enjoyed shoveling the coal from the coal bin to the furnace and watching through the small door as the flames rekindled. My brothers might have done some of this, but I was the main furnace man.

I learned early on that you don't always get the expected reward for extra effort. One of my jobs about age seven was delivering advertising handouts for Straw's Grocery. You took a pre-counted pile of the fliers and a pocketful of rubber bands from Mr. Straw and covered every house over a route of several city blocks around North Main and Randolph streets. At each house, you attached a flier onto the screen door knob. I was so excited the first time that I ran the entire route. I also was hungry and decided to turn the few cents I would earn into something to eat from the store. But when I came back, Mr. Straw couldn't believe anyone could deliver the fliers that fast and accused me of dumping them somewhere. I think I broke into tears, then composed myself and told him he should drive around and check the screen doors. He did and I got an apology and an extra treat. So, it ended well and I had a good little job for a while.

Another job that had a glitch was as a "gazoonie" when the circus came to town and set up in Athletic Park. Don and I hung around the grounds throughout the performances – that's what a gazoonie does. After the last show, the announcer asked on the PA system for all boys 12 and older who wanted to make 50 cents an hour to stay and help tear down the main tent. I was 10, but that was a technicality. Don and I joined the crew, which consisted of "marks," Billy Bigelows, barkers, carnies, and roustabouts – as well as gazoonies. What a bunch of misfits. The big tent came down and as we began to roll it one of my shoes came off and disappeared into the canvas. I shouted out, trying to stop the process, but the other 20 or so pushing the roll did not seem to care. At the end, the circus managers told me I was too young and didn't pay me anything. Don and the others were given 50 cents each, though the job took two or three hours. Some of the big guys almost rioted. I remember limping home in the middle of the night without the shoe or anything to show for it. Someone probably discovered it in the next town. I decided right then I did not want to ever run away with the circus.

Our family did have a run-away once. In the spring of 1951, Helen decided she was ready for professional life and walked down the street carrying a small suitcase. She was in eighth grade. Her goal, it turned out, was to head for Pittsburgh, from where she planned to go on to New York City and join the Metropolitan Opera. I didn't know her plan, but observed her departure with some interest. Like a sleuth in a James Cagney movie, I shadowed Helen through town to the Greyhound station, where she climbed aboard a bus. I ran all the way home to tell Momsy. She was in total shock. When she regained her composure, Momsy called Greyhound and found out which bus Helen was on. A call to Pittsburgh and police were waiting for Helen when the bus arrived. I asked Helen about the incident as I was researching this book and she joked, "In hindsight it was a good thing the police were there. … Otherwise, I probably would have ended up a street urchin in Pittsburgh."

Why did I so quickly tell Momsy of Helen's mad dash for freedom? I think it was because I already had a newsman's instincts and had to tell the story to someone. Then, I realized that Helen had no street smarts and would be helpless out on her own. And, I might have wanted to keep her around. Maybe I liked her more than I thought and admired her dedication to music, even if I could not understand it until many years later.

I remember that incident so well because Momsy did something completely out of character. She took Helen to the landing at the top of the open stairway and spanked her with a broom. I couldn't believe my eyes. I had never seen Helen do anything that deserved corporal punishment. And I had never seen Momsy hit anyone, except on rare occasions with her hand on the backside. My recollection is that the broom was punishment for Helen's attempting to run away and that it occurred after she was delivered home. Helen recently told me the spanking was before she left and the reason she did so. She said she had procrastinated that morning and refused to go to school. For some reason, it made Momsy really angry. I never saw such behavior on Momsy's part before or after. I know she regretted it.

Journeys through darkness

We took advantage of that 1942 Plymouth in the summer by heading east to Cook Forest State Park whenever we could. Momsy would set up the picnic items on a table near one of the shelters and let us run off on the trails with the time of dinner the only instruction we needed. After three or four hours of running through the woods – on and off trails – the sight of the picnic shelter was always welcome. Momsy and Helen would be waiting for us. Cook Forest normally was a one-day trip, but on one occasion we stayed all night in the picnic grove parking lot to watch the animals come and attempt to raid the garbage cans. Raccoons were the most successful. We sat in the car with the lights out and waited, some of us dozing off, until we heard a noise by the row of garbage cans several yards ahead of the car. Then on went the lights. It was great fun, but would be frowned upon now by park rangers. The park these days is closed at sundown.

We had another nighttime adventure at Cook Forest. On one visit, Miriam, Don and I decided we needed another hike after our picnic dinner. From the picnic area to the fire tower is about three miles cross-country. Off the main highway, state Route 36, the fire tower road winds through the old forest and back again. It is a one-way loop about four miles total. The fire tower is at the curve of the loop on a flat ridge high above the Clarion River.

It was beginning to get dark, but we figured that, after we climbed up to the main highway, all we would have to do is stay on level ground and we would come to either the fire tower, or the loop road. If we started downhill, it would mean we were headed for the river and that was not good. If you had a park map you would see we planned to use parts of the Hemlock, Deer Park and Seneca trails. We knew them well.

The amazing thing to me was how quickly darkness came and how dark it was that moonless night in the deep forest. We were soon off the trail. It became so dark we could not see an arm's length in front of us. To avoid walking into trees, we inched along with our arms outstretched. Why no flashlight? They were not as easy to come by as they are today. When we set out, we figured it would be pretty easy to stay on the trail and that we would have enough light to see the path ahead.

The three of us stayed together. We knew that was the key to safety. Luckily, the forest floor was relatively flat and we did not fall into any crevasses. I had found a walking stick and used it much as a blind man uses his cane. Feeling my way along; trying to keep heading in the right direction.

If there is a darkness beyond pitch black, we were in it. All we had were our feelers and the quiet sounds of each other's voices. I was beginning to get scared. We knew bears roam in that area. We had seen one crossing a road not too many visits before. Are they out at night, I wondered. The three of us agreed that the best thing was to just keep moving in as straight a line as possible through the thick forest.

Momsy had agreed to meet us at the fire tower parking lot. When she, Helen and Art got there in the old Plymouth, they wondered and worried, with good cause. After a while, Momsy decided to drive to the main highway, do the loop a couple of times, then seek help if we did not turn up.

I have never been happier to see a light than the moment I saw the headlights of a car off in the distance beaming like lasers through the thick trees. The lights were coming toward us, heading for the highway. The illumination was just enough to carve out a path through the trees and brush and we began to move quickly toward what should be the road. We stumbled onto it just as the car approached. It was Momsy. We drove back to the main highway and headed home, a two-hour drive. Momsy didn't say much about our misadventure. I think she commented on the fact we all should respect the forest in darkness and that she thought we served ourselves well by sticking together.

I think for me it was proof that I could keep calm in dangerous situations, and that I could hold my own with Miriam and Don. There was no real leader on that trek through darkness. It was the three of us, together, knowing we were not alone.

Today, many call the virgin forest there the Black Forest of Pennsylvania. The Thompsons who were on that nocturnal hike more than 60 years ago know why.

Things change

Change is among the few things that are certain in life. In 1952, our lives were changed in a big way when Momsy decided to marry William M. Smith (1913-1988). Willie was a great guy who was widowed and raising a son, Roger. Roger was three years younger than I and had led a much more sheltered life, mostly under the care of his aunts and cousins. His mother, Mona, had died of illness when he was five years old.

Willie Smith: took on an impossible task.

Willie was fairly short, about 5 feet 6 inches, and prematurely balding. He had weak vision and never pretended to be more than a modest working guy. A child of the Great Depression like Momsy, he only made it through eighth grade before quitting school to work. Willie had two hands-on hobbies, bowling and farming, and they kept him busy and happy. I don't think Willie knew quite what he was getting into when he surveyed the five Thompson children as their step-father. Helen was 15; Miriam, 14; Don, 13; me, 11; and Art, 10.

God knows Willie tried to be a provider and a father figure. No one could have tried harder. But, save for scholarly Helen, we were a wild bunch. Willie worked in the power house at the American Viscose fiber plant across French Creek from the main city. It was a thankless, dirty job. It did not pay very well. And his rotating schedule did not leave him a lot of time to be chasing us around.

Roger did get special treatment in the new family setting – new clothes, bowling lessons, extra attention at home – but who can blame Willie for that, or Momsy?

Willie was always good to me and did me one huge favor. Baseball. He got together with Jess Maines and put me on the Coca-Cola team in the Meadville Little League. Finally I was in something that could be called organized – structured practices, real uniforms, decent equipment and a nice ball field.

Little League team, 1953: urchin, second player from right in top row; Roger Smith, at left, bottom row.

Change came again in 1953 when Momsy had her sixth child, Craig Allen Smith, who died at birth. Art and I were sent out to stay with my Aunt Ada and Uncle Al Brink on the old Roberts farm near Venango, 10 miles north of Meadville. While Momsy was in the hospital, she had a tough time and had to stay several days. If you sense a guilt feeling I have toward her, you're right. She had a difficult labor when she was giving me birth back in 1941. Circulation was cut off to her right leg and she developed phlebitis. She would go through the rest of her life with what was referred to as her "bad leg," or sometimes her "sore leg." I still don't know how she managed to work as many as three jobs at once – often standing for hours over a stove – with that swollen leg and the limp it caused.

Aunt Ada was short with prematurely gray hair, which she wore in a bun. Ada had a loud voice and was very religious in a conservative way. She used the time she had me in her clutches to drag

55

me to a small country church where she tried to pound some religion into me. The services included lots of shouting, singing and vocal prayer. But Jesus didn't obey her call to come down through the roof and her efforts to win me over to her views were in vain. Uncle Al was more successful at modifying my behavior. He kept a couple of dairy cows. He took me down to the barn the first morning and gave me a hand shovel with instructions to empty the trench behind the cows. When I had finished, he laughed and said, "Jimmy, you're the best shoveler in the world. Just keep practicing." I finally found something at which I seemed to excel. Uncle Al made good use of me the week or so we were there and never let me forget the joke.

The Brinks also had an outhouse because there was no plumbing inside the two-story, wood-frame farmhouse. In those days, a really prosperous farm, especially if there were 10 or 12 children, would have a two-seater. For those who do not know, an outhouse is a wooden structure over a ten-foot-deep hole. The shack, somewhere around five feet square, houses a single bench into which is cut a convenient hole or holes in which to take care of toilet business. I think Uncle Al and Aunt Ada had a one-seater. The Sears Roebuck catalog or old newspaper pages made adequate toilet paper. Some would hang the catalog from a hook so as to keep it dry and in easy reach. I got used to this system very quickly. There was no choice. I also learned how to prime the pump over the well near the rear of the house. Once primed, you pulled the handle up and down and the pump provided a flow of water adequate for basic household needs. You literally bathed in a bucket at Aunt Ada's.

The Brinks were always willing to help Momsy. Cousin Ted Brink told me a few years ago that their Santa Claus during the lean Depression years on that farm was my father, Donald C. Thompson, red suit and all. Other family members have told me that my father also had saved the farm from sheriff's sale back in the 1920s. Cousins Gloria and Joann Brink were my babysitters during the early years on North Main Street. I don't think Momsy had to pay them much.

Technique of calling cows

In contrast to the Brinks' farm was the farm of Aunt Grace and Uncle Charles Schlosser. Grace and Ada were two of Momsy's four sisters. The Schlosser farm was near Mosiertown, as was the Brink farm. But the difference was dramatic. The Brinks were at the top of Gospel Hill, where the land was not very fertile. Uncle Al always had other jobs and didn't want to be a full-time farmer. They grew and baled hay, kept a few cows and chickens, and had a large vegetable garden for family needs. Grace and Charles had their large farm a few miles away in the bottom land east of Cussewago Creek. They seemed to me to be very prosperous, with a large dairy herd, though I never knew how much money they made. Uncle Charles had started out as a teacher in a one-room school. At some point, he decided he would have an easier time controlling cows than children. While Uncle Al was short and balding in the front, full of jokes and merriment, Uncle Charles was tall, thin with sharp features and gray hair. He truly loved to farm and took it very seriously. Many of my classmates know his son, R. Blaine Schlosser. Cousin Blaine was the Crawford County agricultural extension agent his entire working career after he received a degree in agriculture from Pennsylvania State University. Blaine, in retirement, worked with our MASH classmate Calvin Ernst on development of advanced seeds for growing grasses and plants, and for production of wood pellets for heating. Calvin is very well-known and respected internationally for his work in advancing agriculture.

The Schlosser farmhouse was a white two-story with large trees in the yard. A white fence lined the dirt road out front. The large barn across the road from the house was painted red and was adjoined by one or more large silos. The sheds and garages were painted red, as well. It was a picture-book farm.

Aunt Grace had two stoves in her large kitchen. One was wood-fired and used only during canning season. The "new" stove burned gas. I'll swear that at one time there were three stoves in that kitchen, but no one else seems to remember that. I thought two of them were for canning. Canning was certainly a big thing for Aunt Grace. She was round in face and body, somewhat like Momsy, but with an even bigger smile. She loved her role as a farm housewife and played it all day every day. It is hard to imagine Aunt Grace appearing anything but happy.

In back of the house was a large strawberry patch. We would drive out each June to pick berries. I seemed to eat more than I put in the basket, but I did get a nice haul after my appetite was satisfied. Aunt Grace would then reward us with her homemade strawberry shortcake. It was beyond compare. And we would take some berries home, too.

One summer, Don and I were asked to help Uncle Charles bale hay. Blaine was off at school. The bales back then were rectangular and weighed about 80 pounds each. Our job was to lift the pre-formed and tied bales onto a tractor-pulled wagon. That probably was the hardest physical labor I have ever done. I found an excuse the next year to skip that part of farm life. And Charles soon acquired an automatic baler.

Elsie, one of the Schlosser children, was near my age and decided to show me how to help with the dairy business. I quickly discovered I had absolutely no talent for milking cows. Luckily, Uncle Charles had a new-fangled automatic milking machine that did most of the work. Elsie insisted I should do something and took me out to a gate in the pasture fence to call the cows in. I had no idea how one would do that. The herd was not in sight. Elsie explained that you simply called out "Ca-Boss!" and the cows would come. The lead cow had a bell around its neck so you would know when they began moving. I called "Ca-Boss!" Nothing happened. I called "Ca-Boss!" We waited. "OK," Elsie said after several failed attempts on my part, "Let me show you." She climbed up on a rung of the gate and shouted out "Ca-Boss!" just once. The bell sounded immediately in the distance. A few minutes later the cows marched over the crest of the hill and toward the gate at their slow but steady pace. One by one, the milkers followed the leader through the gate, across the road and into the barn where the milking stalls awaited. I think my lesson from Elsie was that in some things you have to know technique in order to obtain good results. I have not tried to call cows in since.

During one visit, Uncle Charles sat me down in his gray Ford and said we were going to Mosiertown. Mosiertown is a village about two miles north of the Schlosser farm. It then had three or four businesses and 20 or so houses. One business was Cal Kleckner's General Store. Inside the two-story block building was a large, dark room with a wooden floor and a long wooden counter in front of a row of shelves lining the wall. In the center of the room was a free-standing, wood-burning, pot-belly stove. Around the stove were five or six chairs with a farmer in overalls sitting in each – save the one being reserved for Uncle Charles. He pulled up a barrel for me to sit on and joined in the conversation. It was about the weather, the price of cows and pigs at the county livestock auction, the weather, how certain crops were doing, and more about the weather. I was greeted briefly by the farmers, and then ignored. I just sat on the sidelines and listened. I have never been in such congenial company. Each took his turn to speak. Not one unpleasant word was uttered. After a certain amount of time – at least half an hour – Uncle Charles, as on cue, got up, walked to the counter, ordered a couple of farm and food items, and we left. When I said he drove a gray Ford, I meant a sedan. He also drove a gray Ford tractor. Both were housed in a barn-garage a short walk from the farmhouse. The car, the tractor and other farm equipment were always clean and well cared for. I asked Uncle Charles why he had a car and tractor painted so much alike. "Once you have a good thing, there's no reason to change," he replied.

Back then you got a new Pennsylvania license plate each year. They were made by state prison inmates. The color scheme rotated from yellow on blue to blue on yellow. Uncle Charles nailed all of his expired plates to his garage walls. There were quite a few. A lot of people did that. I always wished I could get my hands on his collection.

April Fools' joke that wasn't

Don came running into the back bedroom just before 8 a.m. on April 1, 1954. "The house is on fire," he screamed. "Get up!"

I rolled over and told him that I wouldn't bite at an April Fools' joke that silly. Then I noticed the smoke rolling in beneath the bedroom door he had closed behind him.

I never dressed so quickly in my life. Don made one effort to go back out into the upstairs hallway of the eight-room house. But the smoke and heat drove him back into the bedroom and he wisely shut the door. We climbed out a window onto the porch roof and shinnied down to safety. Neighbors were running to the scene. Don and I stood in the back yard for a minute or two, then made our way around the house to the front to look for the others. Smoke was pouring through every opening. Every room seemed to be ablaze, downstairs and up.

Out in the front yard we found Momsy, Miriam and Art, standing with looks of terror on their faces. Art was in his underwear. We watched with that surreal feeling that this is happening, but couldn't be happening. Willie appeared from the upstairs front bedroom window holding Roger in his arms. He ran to the edge of the porch roof and hesitated only a moment before jumping, his nightshirt flowing in the breeze before he made a not-so-soft landing on the hard ground with Roger still in his arms.

Helen, who had years before turned the sewing nook at the top of the open stairway into a bedroom, was last out, coming through her front window. Flames leaped from the window, which was 10 feet behind her, scorching her nightgown and hair as if to engulf her. She panicked and was afraid to jump to the ground 15 feet below. We all called out, "Jump, Helen, jump!"

From the growing crowd of onlookers came a guy we knew only as Red from Sanderson's Barber Shop down on North Street. He was a big man and assured Helen he would catch her. Another singe or two and Helen jumped. He sort of caught her, but both hit the ground.

All nine people were now out of the burning house. A couple of cats perished. The firemen were beginning to arrive. After watching for a few minutes, I didn't know what to do, so I decided to walk up to First District School and join my classmates. I think I was looking for a setting safe and familiar. I didn't realize that I was in shock. The family came and got me a while later. I had grabbed my school books when fleeing the house – but in my haste to dress, had forgotten my socks and my eyeglasses. I relied on those glasses as I was very near-sighted, but the shock gave me 20-20 vision for an hour or two that morning. The Lions Club, as usual, came to the rescue within a day or two; as did the Salvation Army, which brought clothes and food items.

The firefighters took Helen to Spencer Hospital, where she remained a day or two with second-degree burns to her upper arms, back and face. The *Tribune* story said she also sustained contusions to the abdomen in the leap.

The newspaper had the story on Page One, but got some names and facts wrong. What the reporter really missed, however, was a great news story behind the obvious one. House fires are fairly common. Heroism is rare.

Flames Rout Six Local Residents . . .

Three persons were injured as six had to jump from flaming second floor of W. M. Smith residence, 787 N. Main morning. Fire and smoke billow from upper story moments after alarm was sounded.

Fire at 787 North Main Street, April 1, 1954.
Photo by Skillen Studio.

Don was a hero that day. He was in the kitchen when the fire started in the front hallway beneath the large open stairway. One of the first things destroyed was our phone. While Momsy ran across the street to call the Fire Department from a neighbor's, Don ran into the hall and through leaping flames up the stairway to awaken the four of us still up there. He saved our lives that morning. That was the big news story.

I always tried, as a police reporter years later, to talk to those involved in tragedies while at the scene. It is amazing how much more informative the stories usually are when you have input from victims and witnesses, in addition to the official reports from fire and police officials.

The fire at our house started when a three-year-old boy Momsy was babysitting arrived for the day and took off his coat in the hallway. As she walked toward the kitchen, he innocently waved his scarf over a small gas stove and the scarf caught fire. He threw it under the stairway and ran after Momsy, crying. Miriam and Art also were downstairs. They all saw the hallway and stairway in flames, but their attempts to quell it were hopeless.

It took the firefighters hours to get into the house and douse the fire. The exterior had been covered with light-green asbestos shingles a couple of years earlier. The flames did not burn through the shingles, but black smoke billowed continuously from the windows and attic. The house was gutted and a complete loss. I lost everything I owned. Even my catcher's mitt. But my bike was outside and spared.

The largest room in that house was the downstairs library. In it Momsy had stored all of the papers, books and furniture from my late father's law office and his private library. The boxes were stacked almost to the ceiling. I can remember in my early years sneaking into the library to climb over the boxes over to the corner of the large room where my father's rolltop desk was placed. Beside it was a large world globe on a stand. I had to prop myself up on boxes to play with the globe and explore the desk. The top was not locked. In little pigeon holes were 30 or so No. 2 pencils, worn to within an inch of the erasers, which also were well-used. I guess my dad was pretty frugal in some ways. Must be the Scottish blood. Momsy never knew I went in there. It was forbidden.

Some items were burned in the fire; other's singed and water-logged. Even damaged severely were the glass-enclosed library book cases and contents that must have stretched 24 feet or more along the east wall of the double-size room. The hundreds of books, Momsy later told me, were those of the Huidekoper family library. The Huidekopers, founders of the Meadville Theological School, moved the school west to Chicago in 1926. The family left behind their library and entrusted it, she said, to a fellow citizen with some Dutch blood, my father. Hundreds of precious books were in the collection and all were lost. Momsy said she did not know what to do with the library after my father died. She surely was too busy to give it much thought. I wish someone had come forth and taken the collection off our hands.

Eventually, we would carry all of the damaged goods out of the house to store at Momsy's remaining property – an apartment house at 523 Arch Street consisting of four, three-room apartments. I was embarrassed to be seen carrying those boxes of what I called "junk" to the car. I was still carrying them out months later on the day demolition workers were hurling sharp gray roofing slates off the roof. The house was to be torn down the next day. It's a wonder no one was hurt by the shingles. Years later, I was criticized by Momsy for suggesting that it might have been better if our home had burned to the ground. The Arch Street house was still packed with things recovered from the rubble. I threatened to tie Momsy to a chair and cart everything away. Miriam overheard and dashed into the room. "If you try, it will be over my dead body," she shouted at me. I made a hasty retreat and the subject did not come up again for a long time.

Ironically, it turned out there was a treasure or two in that rubble. Charred, soaked, but intact was my father's "log book," a large-volume legal book filled with newspaper clippings and documents that he had compiled as he went along in his career. It included family history, local and national events, and some of his personal notes from the 1920s, 1930s and early 1940s. The book is about nine-by-12 inches and two inches thick – more than 200 pages of clippings. It was spared, I believe, because of its thick cover, typical of the bound volumes you still see in law offices.

A sample of the clippings were *Tribune* interviews with Capt. Thompson about B Company going south in March 1936 to help in the aftermath of the devastating Johnstown Flood. Other clippings dealt with civil defense issues, court cases and civic events. This family treasure is now copied and preserved. It made the fire cleanup ordeal finally worthwhile for me.

Also found in the rubble were my father's Knights Templar sword – charred but still an imposing work of art – and his Army bugle and cavalry sword. The latter he used for ceremonial events at the Meadville Armory. Momsy's hope chest also was recovered and has been restored.

Momsy had some fire insurance, but because of inflation not nearly enough to rebuild on the site or buy a new house. We scrambled to find vacant apartments in which to live – at the Arch Street house and elsewhere. It was difficult. We moved five times over the next five years.

At first and for a long time, we Thompson children concentrated on the fact we all survived. We were young and used to making the best of the situations in which we found ourselves. Life went on. Only in my old age have I reflected on how that fire changed each of our lives forever.

For Momsy, it also was reliving a nightmare. As a little girl on the Roberts farm on Gospel Hill, later the Brink farm, she watched as the farmhouse burned to the ground after being struck by lightning. She told us the family, which included six children, had to live in the chicken coop for the months it took Milton and Sadie Roberts and their friends to rebuild the house.

In our fire, any hope to have a "normal" family household went up in flames and black smoke. After that it was a series of apartments in Meadville, a year in Slippery Rock – my sophomore year of high school – and a return to Meadville where it seemed necessary for me to find a job at age 15 to help make things work. Other than right after the fire, our full family never lived together again as a unit.

The city was our playground

As children, our playground was the entire city of Meadville. Most of my friends had a designated park among the six or so in the city. But with our central location on North Main Street and our freedom of movement, we Thompson children simply picked our playground du jour.

Each summer's day was a blank page, waiting to be filled with adventure. The most convenient park for the Thompson children was Shadybrook on upper North Street, straddling Mill Run. We could cross neighborhood yards to Garden Street, go through the dark tunnel beneath Brooks Brothers Garage and work our way up the stream from the east end of the block-long tunnel, getting only an occasional wet foot. The water was cool and inviting, but too shallow for a swim. Knee-deep was about as good as it got. The playground was well-equipped for that era. We had swings, teeter-totters, climbing bars, basketball courts, crafts, even horseshoe pits. What more could you want? In the earlier years, Miriam would gather up us three boys and head out with Laddie. We would play at the park for hours.

On the north side of the stream was a softball field and the high school football stadium. I remember watching adult softball games on North Street Field. I thought Zeke Zelasko was the fastest pitcher ever. When I was six or seven, I joined Bantam League baseball. We were truly blessed to have as a coach Bob Garbark from the Allegheny College Athletic Department. Bob had caught for the Chicago Cubs and knew everything about baseball. I decided I wanted to be a catcher, too, so I would be in on every play. We were given caps and shirts by various sponsors and wore them all the time – even off the field.

In the Little League, ages 10 to 12, we were given full uniforms, new equipment and a very nice place to play on the ball field on upper Park Avenue behind the Odd Fellows Home. The new Allegheny science building now stands on that property. We fielded six or eight teams. I made the All-Star team both years and began to imagine I was a pretty good athlete. Jim Passilla was then playing Minor League baseball and he showed up at our games when he was in town. One day, after a game, he asked me to stay behind. Jim noticed that I had trouble finding balls popped up over home plate. He hit about 20 for me, then asked, "Can you see the spin on the ball?" "No," I confessed. He told me how important vision was in professional baseball. I realized right then that my baseball career was not going anywhere. Higher-level baseball is not for the near-sighted.

The other ball fields and playgrounds that we frequented were Athletic Park below Water Street; Highland Avenue Park on the hill by the city water reservoir; Huidekoper Park, near Spencer Hospital; Kerrtown Field; and the playground on Lincoln Avenue in the Fifth Ward. For picnics, Momsy would sometimes take us past the Viscose plant to Meadville's Water Works Park on Rogers Ferry Road. It was even shadier than Shadybrook, but had no good playground. The city's current recreation complex on Thurston Road was undeveloped land back then and its development was far in the future. Plans for a new high school at the east end of North Street were not realized until the late 1950s.

The direction we did not take on Mill Run was west, into the two tunnels that extended beneath the downtown area. The first ran from behind the public library on North Main Street about two blocks to an opening right behind Central Fire Station on Park Avenue. The second, longer, tunnel ran from there about five blocks beneath the central business district to the southwest corner of the city near French Creek. These tunnels were dark and scary. I never tried to enter either, though I was sorely tempted. I don't know if that was a sign of good sense, or a lack of courage and a flashlight. Classmate Vito Valella recently told me that he once waded the entire length of the downtown tunnels. He emphasized the word "once."

In winter, we assessed snowfall and ice conditions to determine the best hill for sled-riding on any given day. Allegheny College officials were very tolerant and we had some great rides down the ravine on campus. The hill in front of Reis Library wasn't too bad and the college kids would cheer us on as we bounced down the icy sidewalk. The most dangerous course was the public sidewalk on the east side of North Main Street hill. The ride from campus down to the intersection of Baldwin Street crossed four side streets. We only did this a few times, but had more than one close call when a car came out from one of the side streets as we approached. Momsy didn't know we were doing this and would have been devastated had there been an accident. She gave us a lot of freedom, but did not expect us to be stupid. One time my sled slammed into a fire plug down by Baldwin Street at the foot of the hill. It put a big dent in the front of my sled. Luckily, there was no dent in my head and

I wasn't thrown off and out into the busy intersection. The fire plug survived and is still there.

Playgrounds or other places to play were available outside the city, as well. When I was 10, the Kiwanis Club sponsored all the street urchins it could round up for a week at the Meadville YMCA summer camp on Pymatuning Lake near Espyville. There I met Fred and George Hood, who would become lifelong friends. They lived on a farm on Williamson Road about three miles south of Meadville. With woods, a pond and lots of wild berries to pick, the farm became a very nice playground for Art and me when we were not at camp and were tired of the city parks.

There was a swimming hole with a swinging rope over by Pettis. It was worth a bike ride over there on any hot, summer day, even on dirt roads. The water was about 10 feet deep in the middle of the stream, but we felt we were safe enough if there were three or more in the group.

French Creek was one place strictly off limits to the Thompson children. Momsy said the creek bottom had many holes that would suck you in and trap you in a watery grave. It seems now that her fears were well-founded. That creek has claimed too many lives over the years. She also feared we might contract polio from the creek waters. We took that pretty seriously. I always had the longing to take a canoe down French Creek, the Allegheny, the Ohio and the Mississippi all the way to New Orleans. Then I read about a couple of canoeists who were attacked by robbers while camping along the banks of the Ohio, and I gave up that quest sometime around my early 20s.

Conneaut Lake Park was our special playground. Momsy got a ticket booth job there one summer and we felt we had it made. We couldn't spend the whole day there so we boys would hitchhike out Route 322 in mid-morning, then ride home with her later in the day. The park was to us what Disney World became for later generations – a big wonderful fun-filled playground. The Blue Streak was awesome. The screams of the petrified riders sent shivers down my spine before I ever climbed aboard. I took my first ride as soon as I was tall enough to tiptoe past the minimum-height bar. Miriam probably rode with me. I was scared to death. Clunk, clunk, clunk up the first giant hill, then the "Oh my God!" feeling as it made it over the crest and took off downhill like a bullet. I lost my breath on the first hill, thought I was going to fly out on the big curve by the highway, and didn't regain my sense of composure until I stepped out after the big curve at the end. I could hardly walk. But I was hooked. It was like an initiation into the realm of daring. The other rides were great, too, as was the midway and the free shows they put on near the lakefront.

Going out and back, we had our share of stops at Eddie's Footlong Hotdogs and Hank's Frozen Custard on the Conneaut Lake Road, though most often we could not afford much. Eddie's was founded in 1947; Hank's, in 1952. Both are still in business today, which says a whole lot about the value of quality products and fair prices in business.

Sneaking into the movies

The movies were our dream world and a good part of our entertainment. We had three theaters in Meadville back then – the Academy, the Park and the Mead. Out of town to the west were the Airway and the Lakeside drive-in theaters. Most boroughs had a theater, too, and we would occasionally catch a movie at one of them.

My father was born in 1891 and played several instruments by the time he graduated from Allegheny in 1912. He earned spare money by accompanying the silent movies on the organ or piano at the Academy, the classiest of the three theaters, originally named the Academy of Music. I wish I could have heard him there.

On Saturdays, Momsy would come up with enough money to send Miriam and us three boys to the Mead Theater. Admission was about a dime and you would get a serial short before the cowboy feature. The serials came in 10 or so parts – enough to keep you coming back week after week, but not so many that you might lose interest. The plots were so simple that you could miss a week and still stay up to speed. Each episode had a brief rehash of the previous one and each ended with exciting moments from the one coming next. My favorite serial was "Superman and the Mole Men." I don't think I have to explain that one. Superman won.

It was easy for me to identify with Leo Gorcey and "The Bowery Boys" in their short feature films. The main difference I saw between myself and these Lower Manhattan street urchins was their interaction with more adults than I, and some really tough characters with whom they had encounters. Who can forget Slip Mahoney and his creative use of the English language? A distinguished career came out of his mouth as an extinguished career. Another way to raise movie ticket money was by cashing in soda pop bottles that had deposits. Five bottles returned to the store for two cents each, and you had enough for a ticket at the Mead. The Park and Academy were a bit more expensive.

Tom Mix was my hero before Gene Autry and Roy Rogers rode onto the cowboy scene. Mix was a real cowboy, wounded many times in real gun battles. His films were old, however. He had died in a car accident in 1940. Bob Nolan and the Sons of the Pioneers were in the Roy Rogers movies of the 1950s. Remember the song, "Tumbling Tumbleweeds"? One time the group announced it was coming to Meadville without Roy to play at the Park Theater. I did everything possible to get enough money saved for a ticket. The curtain opened. Bob Nolan was not there. He had missed the trip. I was so disappointed it took a long time to get over it. I guess it was an early lesson that life doesn't always give you what you want, or expect.

In the summer, Art and I, along with Fred and George Hood, would go looking for wild blackberries and clusters of elderberries out on Neason Hill, then head for town when we had a few quarts to sell for movie money. We also had lawns to mow, which also financed quite a few movies.

As teens, we kids would go to a drive-in movie and try to sneak two passengers in – one on the rear-seat floor and one in the trunk. We succeeded a couple of times, and were caught more than once. The theater employees were very understanding, however, and just made you pay for the stowaways.

Two of our very special times of year were Crawford County Fair week and Halloween. The fair has always been one of the best county fairs anywhere. Because I had uncles and aunts who farmed, I enjoyed the livestock tents, unlike a lot of my city friends. Aunt Grace also won her share of canning ribbons. I think my favorite fair activity, besides eating, was to sit on all the new tractors in the dealers' show areas. There were Farmalls (International Harvester), Fords, Allis-Chalmers, Minneapolis-Molines, Olivers, Massey-Fergusons from Canada and the newcomer in our area, John Deere. Most of those brands are now just footnotes in history. Kubota was a Japanese word none of us had ever heard. The tractor dealers let us sit on the tractors, but not start the engines. We rarely could afford the grandstand shows and the midway rides. But it was well worth the long hike up State Road Hill just to be at the fair. I recall that gate admission was very low. That really helped open the fair to everyone.

I did get to drive a tractor once, at about age 12, but it didn't turn out very well. Up on his farm, Charles Hood, or Pap as we all called him, had downed a tree to cut into boards at his sawmill. He and his eldest son, Charles Jr., or Tink as everyone called him then and still call him today, needed someone to back the Farmall up so they could hitch it to the downed tree with a chain. I eagerly volunteered and climbed up on the seat. What I did not realize is that the brake alone will not stop a tractor that is in gear; nor that my left leg was not quite long enough to depress the clutch all the way. I shifted into reverse. I hit the gas and the big red Farmall began to move backward – with power. Before Pap could help me push the clutch in, I had backed the Farmall right up the trunk of a large standing tree, one wheel straddling either side of the trunk. Fortunately, it went far enough that the rear drive wheel rose off the ground and the hit was direct enough that the tractor did not tip over. I would guess I was looking 20 degrees downward. Pap told me to push harder on the clutch. I did and the tractor rolled off the tree. He helped me off. We walked back through the woods and fields to the farmhouse. I was shaken until Pap calmed me down with a glass of his winter cider, "harder than a nail." He only got the cider out of his root cellar on one or two occasions when we were there. The stash was his personal stock and had to last until the next winter.

That's when I learned that Pap, somber-faced farmer that he was, really had a heart. He usually just tolerated us as we played around his farm. We could jump around in the sawdust pile, but knew never to go near the saw itself. The blade must have been three feet in diameter. I should have known before that Pap cared about us. When I was age 10, on a cold, snowy winter day, I convinced Art we should walk across town, up Neason Hill and out Williamson Road to go sled riding with the Hood kids. I had met Fred at summer camp that year. I didn't know how far three miles was, or how far it seems in the midst of a blizzard. We trudged up the hill and walked and walked and walked, pulling our sleds. Only an occasional car went past us. We could only see a few feet ahead. When we got to the dirt part of Williamson Road, we knew we were close. I had never been out to the farm; Fred had told me how to get there. We finally made it, but were too cold and exhausted to walk on a mile or so to the big sledding hill. Pap quietly watched all of this. Art and I didn't look forward to walking back to town. As it grew dark, Pap finally broke his silence. "Get in the car," he said, "I'll drive you home." His old black Buick sedan looked a lot like a hearse, but it was a welcome ride. He never said a word. Just dropped us off in front of our house and got our sleds out of the trunk.

Tink stuck to Pap like glue. The eldest of Pap's four sons, about three years older than I, Tink never went to school that we knew of. And he told me a few years ago that the only time in his life he had seen a doctor was for his military draft physical about 1955. He was given a farmer's deferment. His entire life has been the sawmill, farming and herding Black Angus beef cattle. Pap died several years ago. He and Tink were rebuilding the back porch on their old farmhouse. Pap felt a pain in his chest, sat down on a log, and then fell to the ground, dead. Tink has carried on alone since.

All of the Hood kids made out all right in life. Fred, a high school classmate and just one month older than I, is the one I know best. He enlisted in the Navy after high school. After the service, he returned and attended electronics school and started a television repair business. He worked in the local electronics industry for years and kept up his passion for learning. After several years of work, he earned a degree in computer science at Edinboro University as a part-time student with four children and lots of family obligations. He then commuted to Harrisburg each week to help launch the Internet services of state government. Somehow, he and his wife, Pat, found time early on to build their own two-story, four-bedroom house down the road from the Hood farm. That's doing pretty good for a farm boy who had no advantages given to him.

Halloween costumes for us were home-made and not too elaborate. We had big bags and plenty of energy for trick-or-treat night. It seemed like neighbors who frowned upon our frolics the rest of the year were friendly and generous when we showed up in outfits that did not really disguise who we were. We played no tricks during those rounds. That was the one rule Momsy issued before we ran out of the house. I did pull off one trick in about 1952. The Hudson car dealership was across the street from us. I sneaked over with a bar of soap and wrote on the showroom window, "Hudson Hornet, don't get stung." When you have reached that level of accomplishment, you don't need to do any more. We didn't worry much about treats being tainted, because no one did that in those days. The parade downtown and the crisp autumn air made our Halloweens truly memorable.

It was also the time of year to rake the leaves and burn them at the curb. The entire city was filled with smoke for days after the leaves fell. We didn't think it was unhealthy then, but I am sure it was.

Meadville was and is a beautiful city year-round. In May and June the rhododendrons are spectacular on the Allegheny campus, at Greendale Cemetery, and on lawns around the city. Because of the variety of trees, the fall foliage in the French Creek Valley is a spectacular palette of reds, yellows, oranges and greens. In winter, the snow hangs from the tree branches and covers everything on the ground in a white blanket. The depth of a new snow is easily determined by wading through it. No one worries too much about the cold when the wintry scene is so beautiful.

Meadville's Melting Pot

My mobility and relative freedom gave me more than the average number of playmates. And they came from different neighborhoods, economic circumstances and ethnic backgrounds. In the immediate neighborhood were Donnie Riddle (he wasn't called Spider until much later), Kenny Eddy Ingols and Edgar "Sonny" Fox.

The boys in whose homes I played at one time or another during our grade school years included David Smith on upper Park Avenue; Joe Sherry on Spring Street; Mike Buzza, Dale Hardner, Duane Shreve and Tom Henderson on Randolph street; Bob Say on Jefferson Street; Terry Hart and Stephany Higby in the City Hospital area; Dorothy Bowers on Park Avenue; John Willmarth on North Street; and Ed Hines on Chestnut Street. I developed friendships in the Italian-American community – John and Carmella Gionti, Tony Pero, Alex Grippi, Nick Zoria, Vito Valella and Jim Fucci (sometimes my adversary). Then there was Norman Dragosavac and Rodney McDonald and Norman Tysarck in town and the Hoods and Jim Kelso out on Neason Hill. Later, Bill Smith; Joe Perrotto; Bob Buttermore; Joe Rebrassier; Jack, Jim and Mark Findlay; Pete and John Glaubach; and Max Maloney Jr., who has been a close friend since. Occasionally I would venture up to the North End. I recall a session in Jack Williams' house, where the North End kids gathered. Several others among my old playmates are now my lasting friends and that is to be appreciated. If I left out anyone into whose house I ventured, please forgive me. I have a good memory, not a flawless one.

Why list all these names? Well, Meadville, with a population then of about 20,000, was a true American melting pot. When I reflect on the surnames of my playmates, I find Irish, Scottish, English, Italian, German, Polish, other eastern European and a few other nationalities unfamiliar to me. Meadville had few African-Americans. Most of them lived on West Street near the railroad tracks. Housing integration was not here yet. However, Tom Henderson's father was a minister and they lived in a large gray house at the corner of Randolph Street and Highland Avenue. He and I were best friends the few years he resided there. Two of Art's friends, Robbie Wynn and Bill Strickland, also lived in our First District neighborhood. A few African-American families lived on Sidler Alley, between State and Randolph streets. The Hunter family lived out on Alden Street Extension on the east end of town. Maurice, Raymond, Tommy and Bobby Hunter were among our playmates at Shadybrook Park and they all were good friends and very good basketball players.

The discrimination I recall was between white Catholics and Protestants. The kids who went to one of the two Roman Catholic grade schools, St. Brigid's and St. Agatha's, didn't play too often with Protestant children, or vice versa. Those Catholics who went to the public schools, however, mingled freely with everyone. The YMCA and YWCA were the ultimate melting pots for any ethnic or religious barriers. It didn't matter there who you were, or who your parents were. It was how you played the game.

George and Irene Schroeder bought a house on Garden Street in 1950. To me, the Schroeders were the All-American family. I soon became the neighborhood orphan who would pop in to play badminton with Carol, who was my age; and later, basketball with young George, about four years my junior. I like to pretend I taught them all they know about those sports. I could get away with calling Mr. Schroeder "Schrade" and Mrs. Schroeder by her first name. I admired the way she disciplined her children and kept such an orderly home. One day in the spring I showed up in jeans and no shirt. Irene gently scolded me and said I would catch my death of cold. Then she sent me home to put something more on. She couldn't have known I had no clean shirt to wear. I think I found a lightly soiled one in the wash and returned to their house a little warmer.

Mr. Schroeder had a good job at Talon and was able to buy a new Chevy every five years. He had a dull, green 1950 sedan, but the coral (pink) and gray BelAir he bought in 1955 was a real pretty car, admired all over town. It was what we called "cool." Cars came with many really neat color combinations back in the 1950s. Dodge offered a three-tone coupe – gray, pink and cream. I kidded Schrade about his Chevy having only a six-cylinder engine when the Chevy V-8 was the rage. He reminded me in his patient way that his six had all the power he needed and saved gasoline over a V-8. Since gasoline was about 25 cents a gallon, I did not get the point about economy. He also skipped a radio in the car. He told me that driving was a full-time job and the quiet encouraged family conversations. Schrade was a very smart man. He later pioneered the car-wash business in Meadville and was very successful beyond his Talon career.

It must be clear to any reader that I longed for a "normal" Ozzie and Harriet Nelson household.

The weekly family comedy, "The Adventures of Ozzie and Harriet" began on radio in 1944 and was on TV from 1952 to 1966. With teen-age sons, David and Ricky, the Nelsons were portrayed as the perfect family in the perfect house in the perfect California community. It was a model to which most of us aspired. I sometimes felt I was the only one deprived of that utopian existence, but know now that most of my friends were, too.

The Thompsons were not to have a television until Christmas 1956, when Momsy bought a used black-and-white set. But I could watch news, comedy shows and boxing by standing on the Chestnut Street sidewalk in front of Bob's Home Radio. The owner, Bob Echnoz, played a television in the display windows for hours each day and had a speaker rigged up above the entrance to the store so the sound carried out to the street. It was as much a community service as a way to advertise. You would always find people there in the evenings, sometimes more than a dozen. I remember almost freezing to death watching a program, but I couldn't bear to leave until it ended. The rooftop antennas in use then only picked up one or two TV stations, so there wasn't too much concern about channel choices – Pittsburgh, Erie, and then Youngstown, Ohio.

An early experience with television advances came in about 1949 when I had my *Erie Dispatch* paper route on the North End. One of my customers was the Perrotto family with a lovely house on Woodland Place. They owned Perrotto's grocery store at the south end of town. Joe Perrotto, a member of the family, was a MASH classmate who later became a good friend. I knocked on the door to collect my money and was asked to wait while the person who answered went to get it. I could hardly believe what I saw across the living room. In a large wooden cabinet was an odd-shaped screen – not quite round, not quite oval – that was producing a TV picture in color. I stood there mesmerized. I quickly finished my route and ran all the way home to tell my family what I had seen. A television picture in color! I did not have a color TV until about 1970. They were pretty expensive even then.

I did have a radio. It was housed in one of those old plastic boxes, about the size of a bread box. If you looked inside the box, you saw glowing glass bulbs, like fat electric candles. These were vacuum tubes, the forerunner of the transistor. When a tube blew, repairs could be fairly easy. The bad tube was the one that did not light up. Transistor radios were not in widespread use until the 1960s. They were so small, about the size of a candy box, that you could carry your transistor around with you. How cool! No one dreamed of anything smaller. But now you can wear your radio on your wrist, or put it in your ear. Computers were still about 20 years away. The Apple I wasn't introduced until 1975. Cell phones didn't arrive until 1993. On the radio at bedtime, Don and I would listen to KDKA in Pittsburgh and WWVA in Wheeling, W.Va. We loved the Wheeling Jamboree. They would play Hank Williams songs. Talk about tear-jerkers.

Saved from a life of crime

My life of crime was short-lived. I know you expected something more exciting. I almost titled this work, "Confessions of a mid-America street urchin." I was saved by the bell, so to speak.

When I was about 12 and feeling pretty cocky, a friend, whose name I shall withhold, suggested we try shoplifting. It was easy, he explained. You just had to look inconspicuous and not stand in one place very long. Murphy's Five and Ten Cent Store was our target. Candy bars were the loot. They were displayed on large, glass-plate shelves and very easy to reach.

I must have looked ridiculous as I lingered around the candy counter the first time. Finally, I made my move. I think it was a Zagnut bar. I slipped it into my pocket and exited the store, trying to walk slowly and look calm and collected. No one came after me. It worked!

We did this a few more times. Ten at the most.

I also was a culprit in the great soda pop theft from the truck parking area of the Saegertown Ginger Ale Company. The company made ginger ale, root beer, and several others among the best soda pop flavors in our area. On Sundays, a couple of us rode our bikes six miles each way to Saegertown, where the trucks were parked in a lot beside the factory, some loaded with cases of soft drinks for delivery the next week. The trucks had locked sliding sides that were intended to protect the cargo, but there were slits at the end of each slide and one could reach in there and occasionally score a bottle of pop without breaking it as you eased it out of the deep wooden crate.

**Urchin in his James Dean 'Rebel Without
a Cause' pose: 1956 MHS Yearbook.**

This was not a lucrative pursuit as the pop
was warm, a railroad security officer patrolled the
nearby tracks and the long ride made it seem like a
small reward for a lot of effort. The officer spotted
us once. We made our escape, but that was it. I
tried to square things later by buying Saegertown
root beer, my favorite, whenever I could.

The Kiwanis Club had given me a YMCA
membership and I fancied myself to be a pretty
good boxer. The weekly boxing matches were
among the most popular television shows. It was
before we had football, baseball and basketball on
the tube. Poor kids everywhere knew that boxing

was important for self-defense, and it also could lead to fame and fortune if you were good enough to get into the Golden Gloves and beyond. Joe Louis, Jack Dempsey and Rocky Marciano were national heroes.

One day "The Man" showed up at the Y. "The Man" was Meadville Police Detective Jack Holt. He stood over six feet tall and had been an amateur boxer of some note. Jack was a real presence when he strolled up and down Chestnut Street, or rode around town in his black, unmarked police car. You didn't mess with "The Man."

Jack offered to give those of us in the gym one-on-one lessons in the small enclosed boxing room. I jumped at the chance.

Jack was a lefty and had a reach far too long for a young boy to defend. He started talking to me as we sparred. He toyed for a minute, then knocked me down with a couple of lightning-quick left jabs. He kept talking as he danced around me, totally in control and fending off my feeble jabs with ease. He said he had heard on the street that I had been shoplifting candy bars from Murphy's. He knocked me down again with a right cross. When I got up, he said he knew my mother and had known my father. "You're from a good family," Jack said. "You don't want to end up in trouble and embarrassing your mother." In a few minutes, he had decked me about five times, but never hurt me or left a mark on my body. Some might call it corporal punishment. I call it a learning experience. I am pretty sure he never talked to Momsy about the incident. I surely did not.

My career in crime ended with that lesson. Jack Holt and I became good friends in 1965 when I was a cub reporter on the *Tribune* and he was police chief. He showed me a picture of an earlier day when he worked for the Secret Service. It was a big ticker-tape parade. He was walking close behind the open convertible limousine carrying President Franklin D. Roosevelt. Pretty impressive.

Jack's special rules of police procedure went beyond curing punks of crime in a boxing room. He told me that he had a seasoned criminal in the city lockup once on a misdemeanor charge. Since the old City Hall had no kitchen, those housed in the wire cages called cells were escorted out to eat. It was a short block through Mead Park and up River Street to the Texas Lunch.

This guy thought he was pretty tough and offered Jack a deal. They would walk the other direction from the park, down to the railroad tracks and duke it out. If he prevailed, Jack would drop the charge. If Jack prevailed, the guy would plead guilty.

"It was an offer I couldn't refuse," Jack told me. He said the accused man pleaded guilty later that day.

Those cages in the lockup contained nothing more than a cot and a toilet. When I went into the police station on my first day on the city beat, Jack gave me a tour of the police department. It consisted of about three rooms on the first floor of the yellow-brick city hall, which was located at the foot of Chestnut Street. The building and the nearby train station were razed for construction of the Meadville Mall in the 1970s. I think that was a mistake.

The lockup was dark and dingy with only small windows and nothing on the order of air conditioning other than a slow-moving ceiling fan outside the cages. Jack led me to a cell, told me to go in, and slammed the door. Then he walked out of the room. About 20 minutes later, Jack came back, let me out and asked if that wasn't the best lesson I had learned to that point in my career as a reporter. I readily agreed, suddenly cherishing my freedom. The sound of the lock clicking shut often came back to me years later when I was covering criminal court sentencings for the *Erie Daily Times*. Many of the defendants would leave the courtroom en route to the county prison. Once you have been locked up, you can sense the feeling of helplessness in the one going in.

Jack Holt had several allies in taming this street urchin. Al Stone had just graduated from Allegheny College and got the job of physical director at the Meadville YMCA. Al and Executive Director Harry Day set out to find boys who needed direction and arranged free memberships for them. Don, Art and I jumped at the chance.

The Y had a social clique in a club called Hi-Y. It was made up of boys from middle-income families, and was a fraternity of sorts. Al created a similar club and called it Ki-Y, since the Kiwanis Club sponsored our memberships. It was for the street urchins. I was elected president. The Y became my second home through my early teens. We could swim, play basketball, take gymnastics classes from Olympian gymnast Walter Gaedecke, and, in today's lingo, "hang out." It kept a lot of us out of trouble.

Gaedecke, who had been a member of the Olympic team from his native country in eastern Europe – I believe it was Poland – tried to make gymnasts of us. He had the patience of Job. I was too bulky to be any good. I was OK on the parallel bars, but a loose cannon on the rings. A large frame is not an advantage in gymnastics.

Al Stone knew how to recruit real talent. When I started to attend summer camp at age 10, Ray Cox, the All-American swimmer from Allegheny, was persuaded to be a counselor and taught us all how to swim in one short week. The steps in the oral syllabus were: "Dead-man's float, dead-man's float with kick, air in the mouth and out the nose, fluid arm strokes, full-leg kicks. It's that easy." After Ray made you a "certified" swimmer – about three days for most of us – you could go farther out in the lake to the big raft. It consisted of a wooden platform floating on several empty 55-gallon drums. The raft was at least 10-by-15 feet and was great for sun-bathing and diving. The water there was over our heads.

Swimmers also could take out the two-person canoes from the small dock in our inlet. They were great fun. We would paddle along the shore of the man-made lake and explore every mysterious place. You were lost to the world in minutes as you paddled along the shore. More than once, we had to paddle as hard as we could for our sheltered dock as we watched summer storms approaching over the lake from Ohio. Pymatuning Lake was created in the 1930s by a dam at Jamestown to control flooding on the south-flowing Shenango River. It is quite shallow and prone to high wave action during storms. No one that I know of ever failed to make it to safety.

Dr. Alfred W. Stone,
Edinboro University archives.

As a counselor at the camp, I later taught swimming, canoeing and archery. They all were confidence-builders for the campers, many of whom, like me, spent most of their lives in the city. In three successive years, most campers moved from the Pathfinder, to Ranger to Pioneer bunk-bed cabins, adding to the feeling of growth and achievement.

The week wasn't complete until you had your big, big campfire on the lakefront, where we sang and shared scary stories. The large fire lit up the faces of the young campers as they listened to the stories. The string of flashlights coming back to the cabins must have looked like a swarm of giant fireflies approaching through the darkness.

Another chilling camp experience was in the shower stall behind the mess hall. If we had a water heater, you wouldn't know it. The water was either cold or ice cold, and many a camper screamed in agony as he took his mandatory shower.

My skills as an artful dodger came into play one day at camp when we staged a hound and hare event. I was 11 or 12. A few of us were chosen as hares and scampered off into the fields and woods that covered several acres around the center of the camp. Minutes later, the hounds were loosed and the hares ran for their lives. One touch by a hound and the hare was marched back to camp as a prisoner. The game ended when all of the hares were captured. It usually took less than an hour.

I decided the only way to avoid sure capture was to get off the predictable path. I ran about a mile and headed into a heavily wooded, lightly traveled area in swampy ground near the lake. There, I found a large tree and climbed up to about the second tier of main branches. The perch enabled me to see the surrounding area and provided enough wiggle room that I could move around the trunk to avoid detection.

Several groups of hounds came by. A few even passed right under the tree. No one saw me. How do you handle success? I just stayed in my perch and let the afternoon pass, not knowing the hounds had long ago given up. I decided it was time to go back to earth only when I heard Mabel "Cookie" McNamara ring the dinner bell. I ran all the way back to camp and was greeted outside the mess hall by a pretty decent cheer. I don't know of any other hares who ever escaped the hounds.

Every day at camp began with a recording of "Reveille" and ended with "Taps." The flag on our small parade ground was raised and lowered each day. For many of us, the discipline and order were new experiences. Memories of camp lasted for months with the hope you would be lucky enough to go again the next summer. Very few campers ever became homesick.

Al Stone made me a junior counselor at the Kiwanis Camp when I was 15. So I got to spend the whole summer season out there. The next year, he appointed me chief counselor. I was only 16. It gave me my first real sense of responsibility. That fall, I was hired as a non-certified lifeguard at the YMCA pool. It was mayhem on Saturday mornings, but I never lost a kid. It's a good thing, too. Even then, Red Cross certification was considered a must for any lifeguard.

When the YMCA sponsored a bus trip to Washington, D.C., Al stopped me in the hallway and told me I could go if I agreed to be a counselor and help look out for the younger boys. It would be a free trip. We stayed in the barracks campground near the Jefferson Memorial and the tidal basin. I believe the campground was in East Potomac Park. We got to see the monuments and visit the Smithsonian. The trip was only a couple of days, but it had a profound effect on my life and my belief in the blessings of our freedom and democratic government.

No one was more of a father figure to me than Al Stone. He gave me all those opportunities to be a leader. He inspired me to work hard at school and to attend Allegheny. Al, himself, came from humble beginnings. His father ran the Maytag repair shop on Garden Street. Al lied about his age to get into the Merchant Marine during World War II. He told me once of a supply mission in the South Pacific during which three of the six freighters in the convoy were sunk by Japanese submarines. Al, luckily, was on one that wasn't. After several years at the YMCA, he joined President Lyndon B. Johnson's War on Poverty and ran the Meadville anti-poverty office – Crawford County Community Action Committee – in the mid to late 1960s. Al along the way earned a Ph.D in psychology and was hired at Edinboro State Teachers College, now Edinboro University of Pennsylvania, for what became a highly successful teaching career.

Late in his life, Al invited me to his house and kidded me about the two of us being the only liberals to come out of Allegheny (though I think of myself as one of the lost breed once called Eisenhower Republicans). Al was not really a welfare-state liberal, either. He insisted on hard work and accountability from all those whom he guided at the Y and from those who received benefits in the Great Society programs.

All-around (town) athletes

During my childhood, I lived and breathed sports. Most boys were so occupied, but not to my extent.

From the days Bob Garbark taught us the fundamentals of baseball through the end of the last volleyball game in high school, sports were a year-round activity for me with no down time from one season to the next. That's because for most of those years I was the perfect tag-along for big brother Don. I was always willing to go; didn't mind some time on the sidelines; and was not afraid of the guys I was playing against, most of them two years older than I. I was large for my age and could pretty much hold my own. Don told me recently his biggest failure in life was not pushing me hard enough to become a professional athlete. He certainly tried.

Kenny Eddy Ingols had a basketball court in his back yard on Garden Street. The neighborhood gang learned to play on that court and younger players were always encouraged to show up and try to get into the game. Basketball flourished in the playgrounds, in intramural sports at the grade schools and at the Y.

Baseball requires lots of practice. After I built my bike, Don often would lead me over to Kerrtown Field. There, you could shag fly balls to your heart's content – and we did. Besides the city leagues, Little League and County League, we had pickup baseball games whenever we could assemble enough players to make it interesting. We all wanted to be Major League stars some day. None of us made it.

Football started in summer and followed the fall season until it was too cold and snowy to even try to throw the frozen ball. Our fields were created on the side yard between First District School and the vocational school on North Main Street; the old Montgomery Field at Allegheny College, when the college officials would let us play there; and other makeshift fields in back yards and parks.

Before there was the NBA, there was Vic Kress' driveway near the top of Arch Street hill. That was the height of competitive back-yard basketball. Don and I would walk up there once in a while and occasionally I would even get into the game, although I was a runt by their standards. In other settings, I was usually the top player, or one of them.

One time while we were playing football between the schools on North Main Street, a younger guy approached and asked if he could play, but we sent him home. He was new in town. His dad had opened an insurance office on Randolph Street. We didn't realize that this little kid would go on to become a high school star at Cathedral Prep in Erie, then an All-American at Notre Dame, and then an All-Pro with the Green Bay Packers. We missed our chance to tackle greatness. He was Mike McCoy.

We were spectators, too. I remember sitting on the deck, my legs dangling over the edge, of the "bandbox" gym at the old Meadville High School, watching the likes of Willie Joe Hunter, Lloyd Sharrar, the Jenkins boys, Dale Van Horne, Norman Voorhees and Lloyd Eubanks perform. The floor-level seats accommodated only a few hundred people. The deck surrounding the gym was primarily for a running track. Many old gyms were

97

designed that way. To watch the games from that perch put you right on top of the action. Visiting teams hated to play in that crowded madhouse. In the mid-1950s, the Bulldog games were moved to the new David Mead Fieldhouse at Allegheny, a neutral setting with plenty of seats, but not as much fun for the spectators.

Don, Art and I would catch a few Allegheny football games, too. We would hide our bikes near Robertson Field on North Park Avenue, then sneak in under the fence along a row of pine trees on the visitors' side early in the game. Once under and in the trees, we would pick our moment to sprint down to the bleachers and mingle with the crowd.

I am sure they could see us from the press box across the field and get a good laugh. We were not worth apprehending, but we were serious about the games. Allegheny had an All-American running back, Jim Villa. He played from 1955 to 1958 and was our hero. I still see him occasionally at the Elks Lodge in Erie. I think he could make the team today.

After some of the games, the college would host cider and doughnut parties back on campus in front of the Student Union, which was across North Main Street from the main campus entrance. We would get in line and try as hard as we could to look like college guys. More often than not, we got our cider and doughnuts after a little friendly questioning about what fraternity we belonged to.

My freshman year at Meadville High School was great for me. I was elected to Student Council, was starting center on the Junior High basketball team, and a linebacker on the Junior High football team. In the classroom, it was college prep with high grades all the way.

Meadville junior high basketball, 1955-56; urchin, top row, third player from right. MHS Yearbook photo.

But family circumstances caught up with me again. Momsy, who was living apart from Willie Smith, decided to move us to Slippery Rock in Butler County. It made economic sense, to be sure. Helen was off at college in Edinboro State Teachers College. Miriam was enrolled at Slippery Rock State Teachers College and Don planned to go there the next year.

Momsy rented an apartment in Slippery Rock Borough and got a job in the college cafeteria. I was hit by the Asian flu that winter of 1956-57 and thought I was going to die. Quite a few Americans did die during that outbreak. I played varsity soccer and basketball at what was known as the "lab school" for the college. The kids there were wilder than those in Meadville. Of course I followed Don into action with the wildest of them. Highlights were a ride in the back of a pickup truck at high speeds with no lights on after a Halloween

99

trick; and traveling over 100 mph for the first time – with Charlie McClymonds in his 1955 Chevy. I was going back to dumb in terms of reckless behavior.

I sort of realized that I was backsliding after a night when a group of us attacked a teacher's house with tomatoes from across the street. To our surprise, a state trooper pulled up and we took off running through a corn field. He didn't chase us, but did fire a warning shot into the air. Oh, oh! I never ran so fast. We circled a long way and sneaked back into town from another direction. Pretty clever, but the law outsmarted us that night. Officers went around to the homes of "suspects," and found some of us were not there. The next day at school, our principal, Dr. Joseph McClymonds (not related to Charlie), called us one by one to his office. I think I was first because I was younger and more likely to squeal. I took the Fifth. He took out his paddle. I didn't snitch, but I didn't sit down in comfort for a couple of days. I don't know what happened to the other guys. Nobody, not even Don, was talking.

That winter, I set pins at the Slippery Rock bowling alley after Art led the way. He was only 14. You didn't escape from pin setting without lots of bruises, especially on your legs. But it seemed like good money at the time. For those born in the modern era, a pin setter perched himself on a shelf in the pit at the business end of the bowling alley.

He would jump down and manually set the 10 pins back up after each bowler finished a frame. When the ball hit the pins, they scattered every which way. You learned quickly how to dodge to minimize pain and injury.

Slippery Rock varsity, 1956-57 Yearbook photo.

JIM
THOMPSON

. We were so poor that year that I did not have much of a wardrobe. When one of our classmates, George Drake, was killed in an auto accident, I had to borrow a sport jacket from a guy four inches taller than I to attend the funeral with some semblance of dignity. Everyone liked George. The funeral home was packed. At MASH in 1959, we lost classmate Terry Darrow when he struck another car with his family's brand new '59 Pontiac Bonneville at high speed out on Harmonsburg Road. The death of a classmate is hard to take when you are young and fairly innocent, and still harbor thoughts of immortality. Terry's death did make me a more cautious driver.

Slippery Rock High School had plenty of student teachers from the college and was not nearly as challenging as Meadville High. After my sophomore year there, I begged Momsy to move back to Meadville so I could get a better education – and she finally agreed. Don got a summer job working at Armco Steel in Butler and Miriam was working at the College Grill. It was clear they could make it on their own. I hitchhiked over to Butler with Don that spring and told the hiring boss at Armco that I was 18. He just laughed and told me to beat it. I was 15.

Working my way through high school

Back in Meadville, money was really scarce and I felt I had to go to work. Willie, now back with Momsy, helped me get a dishwashing job at Gray's Restaurant on Market Street before my 16th birthday. Soon after, Al Stone made me chief counselor at the YMCA camp, which was only a summer job. Then I returned to Gray's where I would work for the next four and a half years.

I didn't even get laid off when the restaurant was converted to The Lamplighter Room. Bud Gray, the owner, had me pounding nails and painting furniture during the renovations. It reopened as a very fancy steakhouse. Bud put in a piano bar and had a large mural painted behind the main bar, graced by faces of the city's business leaders. Local artist Alfonso Fugagli had his paintings hanging on all of the walls, which were covered with red velvet wallpaper and illuminated by pretend gaslights on cream-colored standards. The seats in the booths were plush; the waitresses dressed in glossy black uniforms with white aprons. The bartender wore a white jacket and bow tie. It was very high class for Meadville.

I started as the dishwasher, 4 to 10 p.m. six days a week. I soon graduated to salad maker, then added the role of stock room manager, then assistant to Chef Harry Wehler. He was a genuine German chef in his 70s who had worked around the world on cruise ships. He called me Stimpson because he could not pronounce Thompson. I was listed as assistant chef by the time I graduated from high school. But, technically, I was assistant to the chef. You need credentials to wear the white hat. The restaurant job served me well because I could eat there and place my school books on a shelf with one of them opened to a study page. I got a moment of homework in each time I passed by.

I also did various jobs for Johnnie Cocolin at Johnnie's Drive-In on Washington Street, including cleaning the place every morning. Miriam usually was behind the grill in the afternoons and evenings. I also hung on as an inserter at the *Tribune*. The hot-lead press had a capacity of 24 pages as best I can recall. On Thursdays, and before holidays, the advertising sales were greater and an insert of four pages or more was printed ahead of the main press run.

A small gang of street urchins was called in at about 2:30 a.m. to slide the 15,000 or so inserts into the 15,000 or so papers after they came off the press. The work was tedious and required dexterity. One night as an inserter I wrote my first and only song. It was to the tune of Harry Bellafonte's "Banana Boat Song," which went:

Day'o, day'o
Daylight come and me wan' go home
Day, me say day, me say day, me say day
Me say day, me say day-o
Daylight come and me wan' go home

Work all night on a drink of rum
Daylight come and me wan' go home
Stack banana till de morning come
Daylight come and me wan' go home.

Mine started with the second verse and went like this:

Insert da papers all night long,

104

Daylight come and me wan' go home.
Work at the Tribune till the morning come,
Daylight come and me wan' go home.

Then the day'o refrain.

Others joined in and it helped us pass the time as our hands became automatons, smoothly sliding the inserts into the papers – 50 at a time, stack by stack, hour after hour.

Among the inserters who showed up frequently were Fred and George Hood, Leon and Leonard Godsave and Dick Brewton. I wish I could remember the others, but I wasn't always all the way awake down there in the bowels of the *Tribune*. An inserter made $2 for the night's work.

Art had started in the *Tribune* mailroom as part of the regular crew in 1957 when he was age 15. Foreman Ralph Gigone usually ran the addressograph machine, stamping the mailing addresses on all the single-sale papers, which were then bundled for distribution. His hands flew back and forth as each paper had to be in place when the address stamp for that customer came down. Dick Allen also did that and he was lightning fast. Dick also was a master of the glue pot machine. It attached mailing labels to individual papers for Postal Service delivery. Many of my classmates know Dick for his successful car repair shop and used car business in Meadville. He's another urchin who did well. I was hired as a regular mailroom worker a while later. Ron Monroe, Ed Morfenski, Ron Booth and Bob Eddy were part of the crew that I can remember, although only about five of us worked at any one time.

About the time I entered my senior year at MASH, I became fly boy on the press. The churning press, which rose to the ceiling of a large room next to the mailroom, picked out every 50th paper and moved it up a notch on the metal belt coming out of the center of the press a foot or two off the floor. That notched paper enabled the fly boy to bend over and pick up 50 papers at a time and alternately stack them on a carrying cart, odd-even, odd-even, about 10 bundles deep.

The press run on a good night took something over an hour. The press, however, was old and prone to sheering pins. The pins held the metal plates on the tubular wheels of the press. When a pin sheered, the press ground to a halt. The pressmen rushed to replace the broken pin. That gave the fly boy a chance to lie down on one of the empty paper carts and take a nap for the 15 or 20 minutes it took to get back into business. At the end of a press run, everyone in the room was covered with ink. I often went to school that way, nourished by a hamburger Johnnie allowed me to make while I cleaned his restaurant.

Two events stick out in my mind from those nights. On one occasion, I was pushing a paper cart loaded with stacked bundles with Ron Booth on the pulling end. We wheeled the narrow carts from the mailroom through an underground passageway beneath Clinton Court to the building on the south side of that street where the trucks waited for their bundles. I could not see over the bundles of papers on the cart and was pushing it hard. The double doors in the passageway just happened to be closed that night. Booth backed into the door with the full weight of the cart against him. What a scream! It fractured his arm. It took him a long time to forgive me.

MHS freshman homeroom 1955-56.

Then one night Calvin Kost, our classmate Pete Kost's father, came running down the stairs into the basement mailroom. Calvin was circulation manager for the *Tribune*. He had been a good friend of my father's and knew Art and I were working there. "Thompson boy, Thompson boy!"

he shouted. I ran over. He directed me to quit the job I was doing and follow him up the stairs. We got into his car and drove all over town picking up the early bundles of papers that had already gone out. It seems that in makeup the day before, the photos of two brides had been accidentally switched in wedding announcements. One was a prominent family and there would be hell to pay if any of those papers were circulated. Calvin and I retrieved them all. He indicated he picked me for the mission because he thought I could keep my mouth shut. I did for a long time.

I can't leave my *Tribune* story without mentioning the Bates family. Bob and Ed Bates were dedicated publishers and journalists. I came to really appreciate them when I was a cub reporter at the *Tribune* in 1965. Ken P. Williams was as good a managing editor and teacher as you could find anywhere. The quality of the paper says a lot for family, rather than corporate chain, ownership of local newspapers. Bob Bates Jr. was Student Council governor when I was on it a few years before and was already a seasoned reporter when I joined the *Tribune*. We had a lot of good times chasing stories.

The only time Bob Bates Sr. looked askance at me was in the spring of 1968. Civil Rights leader Martin Luther King Jr. had been shot to death on the balcony of a Memphis hotel and the nation was in shock and mourning. The Rev. Neal Ferris, pastor of the Unitarian Universalist Church in Meadville, organized a memorial march that would circle Diamond Park and conclude with some remarks on King's accomplishments. *Tribune* editorial writer John "Spike" Siegel suggested that he and I march in the parade. I agreed and we were out front with Rev. Ferris. I noticed that of the 100 or so marchers, only a few of us were white. When we got back, Bob Bates Sr. came out of the publisher's office and just looked at us with a bit of a frown. Bob, I figured, was not upset that we marched in the parade, but that we took on the role of activists when we were to be the observers. I think I did do a story on the speeches and, as always, kept it as objective as I could.

Many of my classmates also worked during high school. I wasn't alone by any means. The farm kids worked all the time. I had enough experience to realize how much work is involved on a farm – every day, all day. In the city, it seems as though classmate Chuck Anderson grew up at the *Tribune,* compiling statistics and writing sports throughout high school and for years afterward. Chuck, or Charlie, take your pick, has since spent his entire life promoting Meadville. No one loves the city as much as he does. In 1965, he helped me get my job at the *Tribune.* Every city needs a Chuck Anderson, but I think they threw away the mold. Another natural journalist was classmate Eric Johnson, who seemed to be attached at the hip to WMGW radio. He was a part-timer at the station while still in high school. He worked with one of my favorite people, Paul Brown. You knew everything was going to be OK when Paul came on the air each evening with the 6 o-clock Avisco News. He was a quiet voice of reason in our community, and later for WQLN public radio in Erie. Eric went on to a stellar career in broadcasting in Erie, first with WICU-TV, then WJET-TV, where he was news director, among other things. He has admitted to me that he used to sleep with his police radio at his side. He never seemed to miss a breaking story. After retirement from television, Eric joined the Communications Division of the Pennsylvania State Police. He's still there and I would not be surprised if that police radio is still at his bedside.

My sisters both worked at Dreisbach's Restaurant on Chestnut Street, as did Momsy at times. The Dreisbach family was very good to us. Miriam later was hired by Johnnie Cocolin to be his second in command at Johnnie's Drive-In on Washington Street. Johnnie's was a favorite hangout for our entire generation – much like Arnold's Drive-In, which was made famous later in the TV sitcom, "Happy Days." Miriam pretty much ran Johnnie's until she went off to college.

Helen and Art got summer jobs at West's Inn at Chautauqua Institution up in New York State. I remember when the Kingston Trio came there to perform and I decided, along with one or two others, to save the $3 admission and climb the fence that surrounded the grounds. It had some barbed wire at the top, but that seemed like a small challenge. We made it all right, but I realized when I hit the ground that I had torn my new shirt on the wire. The shirt had cost me $2.98. Who says crime pays? Two cents?

I also went to Chautauqua to see and hear celebrated pianist Van Cliburn (1934-2013) in concert not too long after he surprised the music world by winning the 1958 Tchaikovsky Piano Competition in Moscow. That Chautauqua performance entirely changed my feeling about classical music. I have no musical talent, but have been an avid listener of WQLN since it began the classics programming 30 or 40 years ago. I guess you can bring culture to the savage breast, Helen would say. This is the same boy who used to throw his father's vintage 78-rpm records around like Frisbees, who broke the crank on our genuine antique Victrola and who harassed Helen each Saturday afternoon as she tried to listen to Texaco's Metropolitan Opera on the Air in her little sewing nook bedroom.

A lot of our classmates worked in family businesses. I don't think most talked much about it. We were a generation with a good work ethic. It was expected of most of us.

Momsy on the hill

Momsy might hold the record for the number of jobs held by any woman in Meadville. She had learned to cook and bake as a girl back on the farm. At Meadville High School she was named to the National Honor Society and took business courses, including stenography and typing. Few girls went on to college during the Great Depression and she had no chance to do so. Momsy' father, Milton Roberts, had died in 1927. Momsy and her sisters took care of their mother, Sadie, who was blind due to diabetes complications, until her death in 1935.

Momsy, after graduation, went to work in the office at Meadville Malleable Iron Company. In the 1950s, besides Conneaut Lake Park and Dreisbach's, I can recall her working for Meadville Cab Co. (yes, she was the first local female cab driver); as a cook for the Crawford County Home, the Meadville City Hospital cafeteria, and later for the summer theater at the Allegheny's Klie House on North Main Street; as secretary for the Theater Arts Department at Allegheny; legal secretary for Attorney Max Maloney; and for several years as a clerk-typist in the Crawford County Register and Recorder's Office. She could pound out more than 100 words per minute on an old Royal. It was fun to watch. She did not get the jobs she should have. I think many potential employers did not believe Donald Thompson's widow really needed a job. Some probably thought she could not perform reliably while raising five children. It was always a struggle.

The most important of her jobs to me was that at Allegheny up on college hill. She had told

Art and me back in 1957 that she saw no way to help us get through college financially, though a college education was her top directive all the time we were growing up. One of the reasons I worked through high school was to save money for college. Allegheny, where my father had graduated in 1912, was high on my list. When the time came, her job at the college got me half tuition on the hill. The Harris Fund in Titusville gave me the other half. I offered Momsy the few hundred dollars I had saved, but she refused to accept it. So, I defiantly went to Erie and bought a new Triumph TR-3 sports car. Not a very smart move for a supposedly smart boy. But I craved acceptance and attention. At the time, I was the poster boy for acne creams and pretty scarred up all over for my age. It was great to drive, but other motorists had trouble seeing the little sports car. I almost got killed in it twice; Art, Roger, Frank Wood and young George Schroeder, once each. Roger and Frank were passengers when Art rolled it over on a curve. He fractured his back in that accident. George and I were coming home from a basketball game in Mercer County when we were hit from behind by a big Buick. I had to junk the Triumph after that accident. I left my sports car years with a 10 percent permanent disability from the damage to my spine. I have lived with the pain ever since.   Momsy's relationship with Allegheny had a note of irony. She worked for a task master in the Theater Arts Department where her boss had her doing menial jobs and kept her on a schedule that included evenings and extended shifts. She did just about everything involved with getting the playshop productions ready, including helping to make the sets, selling the tickets at the box office, and furnishing goodies for post-performance parties. I believe she felt she was badly used at times, and definitely under-appreciated. One or two in the department let her know she was not college-educated.

Allegheny College file photo: Bentley Hall viewed across wooden bridge. Kurt Glaubach photo.

Well, I know something they didn't know. Allegheny was founded back in 1815 by a group from Harvard. That year is commonly used as the founding date. Not so commonly known is that Presbyterian minister Timothy Alden resigned after 15 years, and the founders in 1831 all but gave up on this experiment in a small town on the frontier. The newly completed Bentley Hall housed the library, but no classes. I believe the official history says the college was dormant for a brief period, or something to that effect. My source, "Old Allegheny: A Handbook of Information," by Dallas

Malone Stephens, says for the years 1831-33, "College closed." But he also indicates that the Board of Trustees kept meeting during that period. So I guess one could say the college has been in continuous existence since 1815, but hanging by a thread for two of those years.

During this period of uncertainty, a move by some local residents to make it a military school almost succeeded. That would have changed local history. In 1833, however, the trustees reached an agreement through which the Methodist-Episcopal Church would restart the college as a non-sectarian liberal arts school. The man who presided at those meetings and whose signature is on the transfer papers was Bishop Robert Richford Roberts, head of the Pittsburgh Conference of that church.

Momsy never knew it, but the bishop was the youngest brother of her great-great-grandfather. I learned of the family connection only recently in Stephens' book, and confirmed it in a biography of Bishop Roberts written by the Rev. Worth Marion Tippy – "Frontier Bishop. The life and times of Robert Richford Roberts (1778-1843)." The bishop also gave money personally to help get Allegheny going again, his biographers say. Incidentally, Bishop Roberts' first circuit in 1816 covered 4,000 miles on horseback – all the way west from Mercer County to Indiana and south on the Natchez Trace to Mississippi, then back east to Virginia and Baltimore. He later founded DePauw University in Greencastle, Ind. Roberts earlier brought Methodism to Meadville when he was a circuit preacher, operating from his farm in Mercer County. The first meeting in 1806, according to Methodist historian and one-time Allegheny College vice president, the Rev. Dr. Matthew

Simpson, was in a hotel bar. The first service was in a room above a blacksmith's shop.

Had Momsy's tie to the resurrection of Allegheny been known when she worked there, I think she might have received more respect – perhaps even a "founding family" badge. They could have dusted off the old Roberts Professorship (1833) and let her teach a course – Humility 101, with emphasis in overcoming adversity while keeping your sense of humor. It would have been a good one.

Despite Momsy's experience, I never found the college faculty, administration or student body to be overly snobbish. There were some with an attitude, of course, especially among the "big city" students finding themselves in the boondocks. And "townies" in those days were not always in the mainstream on campus. To me, the professors on the hill were gods. My first advisor was Dr. Jay Luvaas with a PhD in history from Duke and the author of several books on the American Civil War. My second advisor was Dr. Henry Pommer, a Yale PhD and a Unitarian minister. His eulogy of President John F. Kennedy was selected for the national collection of Kennedy memorials. The college had a superb faculty. I think it was a wonder that these academic gods fit as well as they did in this small manufacturing and farming community in the woods of Western Pennsylvania.

Momsy's finest moment on campus might well have been when she saved a student from being ousted from the Air Force Reserve Officers Training Corps. The student was me. The military draft was very real then in the life of each young American male. We registered for the two-year draft, but could get a deferment if we went to college. At Allegheny, the two-year ROTC program was mandatory for male students. We had to wear Air Force uniforms on Mondays, Wednesdays and Fridays, and get passing grades in our ROTC classes. I found the classes to be fairly easy and interesting. We learned about aircraft and military strategy. Many of the finest officers in the U.S. Armed Forces have come out of the ROTC programs. My problem was that I was working lunches down at the Lamplighter Room and had a hard time getting into uniform and up the hill to class on time in the afternoons. I went too far when I missed four ROTC classes in one semester. That was automatic dismissal from the program, and, according to college policy, dismissal from school.

Col. Herbert L. Fleischer, professor of Air Science, had an office in the basement of historic Bentley Hall. I was summoned to appear before him, and walked in with the anticipation of a gladiator heading onto the floor of the Roman Coliseum. Momsy walked over from her office to be with me. I was so nervous I forgot to salute the colonel. Not a good start. I told him truthfully that I had the highest mark in my class on the ROTC mid-term exam. He did not seem to be impressed as he glared at me as if the decision to oust me was already made. I explained about my work schedule and the difficulty getting to some classes. He was not moved. Then, from behind me, Momsy stepped up and told him a little bit about our family history and a proud line of military service going from my father in the world wars back to his great-grandfather in the Revolutionary War. She did a great job, but I think it was the tears that got to the colonel and touched the humanity buried somewhere deep within his heart. "I'll let him go," he told Momsy, "but he had better not miss any more ROTC classes."

It reminds me of the words of sportswriter Grantland Rice in his sequel to the famous 1888 Ernest Thayer poem, "Casey at the Bat." Rice's 1907 poem was titled "Casey's Revenge." It read, in part: "The lane is long, someone has said, that never turns again. And Fate, though fickle, often gives another chance to men." Casey got his and hit a game-winning home run; I had just been given mine.

I didn't know then that I would have another close call before completing my ROTC obligation to the college. Each spring we had a President's Review. Up at Robertson Field the ROTC students would march past the grandstand, on which sat the college president, Dr. Lawrence L. Pelletier, and a host of faculty and dignitaries. The review was mandatory with a capital M.

For the review in 1961, I rushed from work and drove up to the stadium, but arrived just after my unit had marched in. Too late. I had to make a command decision. Recalling the days when my brothers and I circled the stadium to sneak into football games, I calculated which exit the formations would use after they passed in review. I parked my 1952 Plymouth, ironically painted Air Force blue, in a nearby grove of trees – and waited.

I could hear the music through the stadium wall. Soon the first units marched out. I casually walked from my car to the exit gate and stood against the wall, as if on assignment for some general. When my unit marched by, I fell in step at the rear. It reminds me of the scene in the movie, "The Wizard of Oz," in which the lion, scarecrow and tin man use the same trick of blending in with the troops to get across the moat and into the castle, where they will try to save Dorothy and Toto. I had guessed correctly that roll call would follow the review. My name was called. "Present," I shouted. And we were dismissed, unscathed. Had the colonel known about that one, I think he would have come looking for me brandishing his swagger stick and expulsion papers.

One other ROTC adventure was a "town meets gown" occurrence. I finished working the lunch hour at the Lamplighter Room and changed into my blue ROTC uniform. I was late, as usual, and drove that blue Plymouth up Park Avenue hill at a pretty good clip. I found a straight-in parking spot on the street beside Brooks Hall. I grabbed my brimmed Air Force hat and my books. Unbeknownst to me, a city police car had pulled in behind me. At exactly the same time I exited my car and put on my hat, the young officer exited his car and put on his hat, which was very similar to mine, but black. We looked at each other in total surprise. I almost saluted. So did he. He didn't know whether I was a student or a real officer. "Sir, you were going pretty fast up that hill," he said. "I know," I responded. "I have an urgent appointment."

He paused for just a moment, and said. "Well, go slower next time."

I apologized and headed up the sidewalk for class at a pace that would put me out of sight before he could change his mind. He got into his cruiser and drove off up Park Avenue, still shaking his head. Amazing, isn't it, what a uniform can do?

Being somewhat disillusioned with the Air Force, I took a hiatus from Allegheny that spring and joined the Army that fall. I have never regretted that decision. I admire all branches of our Armed Forces equally. The Army promised foreign travel and we were not at war at that time.

Pioneer past

Allegheny was not even dreamed of in 1795 when the first two members of the Roberts family settled in what is now Mercer County. Their land claim was along a branch of the Shenango River a few miles south of the great Conneaut Marsh. Ten miles north of the marsh was a small settlement called Cussewago, founded years earlier by Native Americans. Located at the confluence of French and Cussewago creeks, it had become home to a few white settlers about 10 years earlier. David Mead arrived with others in 1788 and Meadville was born. To attract people to some sections of the western Pennsylvania frontier, the state offered 400 acres of free land if a pioneer built a cabin within five years of arrival and cultivated a specified portion of the land. Others were given land as a reward for service during the American Revolution. I believe the latter is how the Roberts family obtained the farm in Westmoreland County in 1785, as Robert Morgan Roberts had fought in several of the major battles of the war.

According to family biographers, he fought at Brandywine, Germantown and White Plains under the command of General George Washington, and, at times, under the Marquis de Lafayette. He was the young French officer who came to America to help the Colonies battle for independence from Great Britain. Roberts also talked of being at Valley Forge, but this is less-well documented. Roberts, it is said, in 1775 traveled to York, Pa., from the family home in northern Maryland, near Frederick, to have a set of saddle pistols hand-made prior to the war. Those pistols survived generations and were featured on the cover of *American*

Rifleman magazine in its July 1972 edition. Engraved on them are the words "Robert Roberts." They were housed in the Remington Museum in the middle of the 20th Century, but I have been unable to find out where they are now. The magazine article said a family member sold them to an antique shop in Chester County, Pa., and they were then sold to the Remington collection for $450. I would rather they had been stolen or burned in a fire, rather than to be sold for that pittance.

I believe those walnut, brass and iron pistols are every bit as impressive as the George Washington saddle flintlocks I have seen at the Fort Ligonier museum, east of Pittsburgh. Washington's pistols were given to him by Lafayette, according to museum documents. Later, they were owned by General Andrew Jackson, who received them as a gift. In 2002, Washington's were purchased by the Richard King Mellon Foundation for just under $2 million. I doubt that I could even dream of purchasing the Roberts' pistols if I could ever find them.

In 1797, Robert Morgan Roberts' daughter Elizabeth, 25, and two of her brothers made the 175-mile journey from the first Roberts homestead near Fort Ligonier to Shenango to bring supplies and four cows to the two young male family members then homesteading there. Their journey, on foot and horseback, led over the mountains to the Allegheny River; up the trail along the Allegheny to Franklin; across the Allegheny and the mouth of French Creek at Franklin; then on west across the rolling hills to the Roberts homestead near what is now Greenville. I have driven it and that itinerary is my best guess. Elizabeth stayed on at Shenango and is said to be the first white woman settler of

Mercer County. More family members made the transition from the Laurel Highlands to Shenango in the spring of 1798. The party consisted of the future bishop; his brother, Lewis; two sisters, Nancy and Sophia; and their 93-year-old maternal grandfather Richford. He rode while the others walked. It took them 10 days, with some precarious adventures crossing swollen streams with the old man in tow. Nancy drove three cows and two pigs, with an ax on her shoulder. Sarah walked with a spinning wheel on her shoulder, according to the biographies of the Roberts family.

Momsy, had she known anything about past generations of her family, could have claimed genuine pioneer blood. The Thompsons were comparative newcomers, arriving in what is now Union City by river raft in 1801. Abel and Jemima Thompson traveled into the "mountains" from Brownsville (Redstone) in Fayette County on the Monongahela River, where he had been blacksmithing for 10 years. They floated down the Monongahela River, around the point at Fort Pitt, poled up the Allegheny to Franklin, and then up French Creek as far as the raft could go on the South Branch in eastern Erie County. There, they built a cabin and did the blacksmith and mechanical work on the new sawmill and gristmill that had been built there a year before. Unbeknownst to them, the Thompsons either floated by or walked along the same Allegheny River trail the Roberts family had used so often the preceding six years.

It is possible that Robert Morgan Roberts met Abel Thompson during that cold, bitter winter of 1777-78 at Valley Forge, as evidence suggests that Abel might well have been a blacksmith there.

The families, however, never actually met until my parents' generation, as far as I know.

One interesting note about the Union City area is that newcomers shied away from land to the south of the settlement. It seems there was a slick cover on the stream water that made it useless to feed livestock. It rendered the land next to worthless. The mysterious slick stuff, of course, was oil. It wasn't until 1859 that Colonel Edwin Drake down in Titusville discovered how to collect that gooey substance and turn it into a fortune. One of the streams in that area is actually named Oil Creek.

Scholar, lawyer, G-man

Despite the tough schedule, Momsy loved Allegheny, especially the students. She was very pleased that I decided to go there. My father and I actually taught classes at the college 90 years apart. Seem impossible? He taught a history course right after graduation in 1912. I taught an English course in 2002. My father's yearbook note gives him the nickname "Cicero." It reads: "Shirked the price of an Encyclopedia Britannica by committing it to memory. Utilized as a 'Ready Reference in Supreme Court Cases' by Dr. Benjamin. Has a very ready tongue, having a speaking knowledge of French, German, Spanish, Russian, Swedish, Hebrew, Sanskrit, etc. Is planning to do graduate work in Ancient Chinese Literature." Actually, he put off graduate work and apprenticed under Meadville lawyer Otto Kohler. In 1913 he became, I believe, the youngest ever to pass the Pennsylvania Bar at age 21. When he ran for the Pennsylvania Senate in 1920, his ad in the Cambridge Springs Enterprise – which I found pasted in the water-soaked log book – read, in part: "This candidate was born and raised in Crawford County, worked his way through Allegheny College, and later taught on the faculty. ... His heart lies with men who work honestly for a living. Endorsed by the Anti-Saloon League. A Good Roads booster. A thorough student of economics and public welfare. A clean, square, safe candidate." The big issue that year was whether the Legislature would be for banning alcohol, a "dry;" or against banning it, a "wet." My father's ad said he was "a sure dry." No one among all the Thompson family members that I know of ever drank more than a wee bit of alcohol – until it came to me. I was an abstainer until I was stationed at a U.S. Army base in southern Germany in 1964. A summer of Bavarian village fests and one October Fest and I became a beer connoisseur. In today's language, that means a regular beer drinker. I've enjoyed it ever since; better in moderation than excess.

I have been told that my father represented several of the immigrants in the community in legal cases, partly because of his language skills. I recall a time when I was about to graduate from Allegheny and working for the *Erie Daily Times* in Meadville when prominent attorney George Barco stopped me in Diamond Park. He said he had seen my name in the paper among local graduates and congratulated me on making it through school and on my reporting career. He then startled me by saying he would be willing to sponsor me at the University of Pittsburgh Law School, where he was on the board of trustees, if I would commit to work for the Meadville firm of Barco and Barco after graduation. The Barco family also owned our local cable television company, Meadville Master Antenna. But I was in love with journalism and had a family to take care of, so I had to say no. He told me he made the offer because my father many years earlier was the only lawyer who would sponsor an Italian-American for admission to the Crawford County Bar. That was one of the most cherished conversations I have ever had and one of the nicest things ever said about my father. When I think about the offer, I recall the final lines of poet Robert Frost's "The Road Not Taken." "Two roads diverged in a wood, and I – I took the one less traveled by. And that has made all the difference."

126

My father was not perfect, even though Momsy tried to convince us that he had been nearly that. He had married his childhood sweetheart, Bernice Klipple, when a young man. They had a good marriage, from what I have been told, but did not have any children. The two aunts, mainly Edith I believe, insisted that Donald give the family Thompson surname male heirs. That was fairly common back then. Everyone wanted a family dynasty. It was part of the American Dream.

Sometime around 1930, a local tale goes, G-men came to Meadville to investigate a series of kidnappings at Conneaut Lake Park. It seems gangsters from Chicago were scouting the dances for young, innocent, country girls. They kidnapped them and sold them into sex slavery in the big cities. G-man is slang for government man. They worked for the U.S. Department of Justice before the FBI was born in 1935, and were mainly involved in investigating organized crime. When the G-men came to town, they were required to enlist and cooperate with local officials so people wouldn't think Big Brother was swooping down on their towns unchecked.

During World War I, my father rose from company bugler in Texas to military intelligence operations at Fort Meade, Md. After the war, he remained in the Army National Guard, received a commission, and eventually ran the Meadville Armory.

The G-men, I am told, took him with them as the local representative and legal liaison on an armed expedition to catch kidnappers in the act at Conneaut Lake Park. There was a shoot-out, though I don't think anyone was killed, and several girls were rescued. One of them was Sue Roberts, a tall, lanky, vivacious farm girl from northern Crawford County. Sue was one of Momsy's four sisters, Momsy being the youngest. Sue had a way of winning people's hearts with her knowing eyes, quick wit and laughing smile.

The G-men went back to Washington with their captives. My father was sort of stuck with Sue, who apparently did not want to go home. I would not infer any judgment as I know almost nothing of the facts of that period. But I do know that my father divorced Bernice and married Sue, whom, it seems, was temporarily housed in his Titusville law office. He was city solicitor of Titusville for several years, but always resided in Meadville.

Sue also bore no children and she was far too wild for that quiet, modest small-town lawyer who was about as exciting as Atticus Finch in Harper Lee's "To Kill a Mockingbird." The marriage lasted about five years. As he had with Bernice, my father provided Sue with a generous divorce settlement. She went to Cleveland, opened a school that taught guitar and Hawaiian ukulele playing. Sue later settled down and married a Kansas wheat farmer and had a very comfortable and productive life. Sue had introduced Donald to her family, one of them being Momsy, then Laura, and you know the rest.

Sue wasn't happy about the breakup and she and Momsy parted on an unfriendly basis. Momsy for years was paranoid about Sue. She knew Sue was still childless and feared her sister would try to take one or more of her children from her. We had strict orders not to answer the door if a tall, lanky dark-haired woman ever knocked. It never happened, but I did meet Aunt Sue once – when I was 13 years old.

In 1954, a couple of months after our house fire, Sue and her husband, Harry Ek, came to Meadville from Kansas to purchase a new sedan from Wyatt's Chevrolet. Someone arranged for Sue and Momsy to meet. Sue and Harry drove up to the Arch Street house in their shiny new car. As soon as I met Sue, I was fascinated by her. On Sue's part, I think she saw in me an image of my father. Anyway, we bonded immediately and talked and joked a great deal during the hour or so she was there.

The Eks stayed a day or two longer and visited once more. Sue hinted that she would like to take me back to Kansas to help run the wheat farm. I wanted so much to go. But I thought it over for a few hours and decided I could not leave Momsy, especially in that time of need. Sue went home to Kansas. That was it. Momsy and her sister parted as friends. Neither Sue nor Bernice held any ill feelings toward my father that I knew of.

Divorces back in the 1930s were the kiss of death for those with political ambitions. My father made one try for district attorney in the 1930s, but lost in the Republican primary. He had so much going for him, but that was a barrier too high.

When I look at his life as a whole, I think of Donald C. Thompson as one of the last of the breed known as Renaissance men. Webster describes such a person as one who has a wide range of interests and is expert in several areas. These days, one has access to a great deal of knowledge. It is only a computer click away. And then it is used and gone. Back then, it had to be read and digested and stored away in large libraries for use when needed down the road.

I have always regretted not having known my father, other than as a ghostlike figure from my earliest memory. I can vaguely recall once looking through a large doorway at the Alden Street house and seeing him playing the piano. I was about age two. I do know he had nicknames for his five young children. Helen was Pooky Jinks. Miriam was Tinky Wink. Don was Donny Bug. I was Jimmy Beetle. And Art was Dickie Bird. (He was called Dick throughout his early years. His middle name is Richard.). Our father named himself Schnerz Bagel, "The tiger hunter." I can't remember much detail, but I can imagine the fun we had as he chased us around our large house, down the back stairway and up the front one. A relative filled us in on these monikers many years later. I believe the nicknames tell us something more about my father's character.

The closest I ever came to feeling my father's presence after his death was in 1969 when I worked for the Meadville Parks Department while I was participating in a strike against the Erie newspapers. One of my jobs was to paint the fountain in the center of Diamond Park. Every few years, the department drained the fountain pool and workers cleaned and painted the fountain itself. From that perch, I would glance east across the park and see the courthouse. I would turn around and see the Armory across the street from the west side of the park. I imagined my father walking the tree-lined sidewalk between the two buildings about the time I was born, thinking how good it was to be a citizen of a small American city. I am sure he made that walk hundreds of times.

My father had done quite a bit of work in genealogy. Whatever he learned was lost in the fire. He did tell my mother that we Thompson children were a combination of Scottish, Welsh, Irish, English and Dutch. That was our family melting pot. DNA was unknown back then. Had he had access to a DNA lab, a computer and the Internet – not yet invented – he would have found out that on his side we were originally of the MacTavish Clan of Scotland. I have all but concluded that relationship from my recent DNA analysis. I bet he had learned, however, that his great-great-great-great-grandfather came to New Jersey from Yorkshire, England in 1684, an indentured worker for the first seven years, and that the family later had Quaker ties in the Trenton, N.J., area. The Dutch blood came from a 17th century marriage in the "New World."

I noted earlier that my father was not wealthy. I have a group photograph of the 1940 Crawford County Bar. Thirty-nine lawyers. Today, the number is well over 100. Seems there is a lot more legal business these days. O. Clare Kent was the judge back then. Thomas Prather was still active as a semi-retired judge. His son, Frank Prather, and my father had notable chess matches in the courthouse hallway during slow times. They used to kid each other about fathering strings of boy children. Let's see: Thomas, Mark and Bill Prather; Don, Jim and Art Thompson. All in about the same time frame.

The district attorney's office wasn't as clearly defined as it is now. Lawyers would sort of take turns handling the prosecution and defense in minor criminal cases. Clients often had little money, especially during the 1930s. My dad would often barter to get paid, but sometimes the goods did not materialize. Momsy used to quote my father as saying: "If everyone who owes me a hog, a chicken or a side of beef came through, this family would never go hungry."

Momsy and Willie

Willie Smith lived on and off with Momsy in the late 1950s and 1960s. He and I had a warm relationship during good and bad times. His first love after Roger was his five-acre farm five miles out toward Titusville off Route 27. There, we played a lot of catch with baseballs and footballs and I learned to dig potatoes. Spuds tasted better when you knew you had dug them yourself. Willie's dog, Rin Tin Tin, was named after the famed movie dog. They spent a good deal of the time in a nice little cabin Willie built there.

Willie's farm faced Hatch Hill Road. His brothers, Albert and Woodrow Smith, had much larger farms up at the top of the hill, a couple of miles away. One summer evening about 1953, we all decided to go from Willie's farm up to Albert's to watch the boxing matches on TV. I suggested that Roger and I walk up ahead of the rest, who would come in Willie's car. Roger excitedly agreed and off we went. The road curved to the right near the foot of the hill and I got the bright idea we could walk straight up through a ravine and get to Albert's faster. The sun was setting. It began to get dark. The ravine turned out to be more of a thicket than an easy path. We were pretty well lost when darkness came.

After a while I spotted lights in the far left distance. Albert's house would have been to the right. We set out through the ravine and up toward the lights. Any light is promising when you are in darkness. When we arrived at that farmhouse, the family let us in and telephoned Albert's, which was a mile or so to the east as the crow flies, to get us a ride. Back at Albert's, Momsy spanked me in front of the entire Smith family. The spanking didn't hurt much and seemed unfair. I thought of myself as something of a hero for having chosen the smart way to safety. I think Momsy was terrified that something bad might have happened to Roger, and had to make a show of something. I eventually forgave her.

When Willie was dying of cancer in 1988, he asked me to come over to Roger's house, where he was staying. Willie was on the couch and couldn't even sit up. He told me he wanted me to forgive him for not doing more to help raise us. I told him the truth. In my opinion, under the circumstances, he did the best he could. We parted with a warm embrace. He died within weeks.

I can't leave Willie without telling the Christmas story. Willie, at times in his life, drank pretty heavily. He never denied it. A lot of people who work in dirty power plants are prone to drink. I was back from the Army. It was Christmas Eve 1965. I came home from the *Tribune* and prepared for a quiet evening. Roger and I were the only two still living at home – which then was the apartment house on Arch Street. I had one of the upstairs apartments to myself. It was really neat.

Momsy came to me in mid-evening and told me she was worried about Willie and asked that I drive downtown and find him. I parked on Market Street, guessing he would be in the Stag Bar. Sure enough. He was down near the far end of the long wooden bar. The place was dark with only a few customers. Before I could say a word, the bartender placed a boilermaker on the counter in front of the stool beside Willie's. For those who don't know, a boilermaker is a glass of beer and a glass of whiskey, served side by side. Some refer to the beer as a chaser. At any rate, I sat down and proceeded to drink as I gently urged him to come home with me soon.

I glanced aside and turned back to find another boilermaker in front of me. Time was passing. We had another. At about 10 p.m., Dode Beck strolled in. I forget his real first name. We all called him Dode. Dode was a large, strong man a few years older than I who was from the Beck family up on Neason Hill. He had been traveling with a carnival in the summers, operating the Ferris wheel.

Dode walked up to a guy sitting on a bar stool, grabbed him, spun him around and clobbered him in the face. The man fell backward and slid several feet beneath a table. There, his head hit the wall with a thud. I figured he might be dead. For sure he was out cold. The bartender went over to tend to him.

That was the excuse I needed. "Come on, Willie," I said, "Let's get out of here." He did not need more persuasion. We hurried to the door. Dode knew me, so let us pass. I never found out why he hit the guy. But the guy lived. Outside it was snowing and cold. Willie and I got into my car and started to drive home, which was only a few blocks away. For some reason I took an indirect route and drove east on North Street. That took us past Rudy's Blue Star. The lights were still on.

"Jimmy," Willie said, "We should have a nightcap. Just one." I was shaken from the event at the Stag Bar and didn't want to argue any more, so I pulled over and we went in. Rudy was happy to have a couple of customers that late on a Christmas Eve. He chatted with us over a couple of boilermakers, then told us we should go home or we would miss Santa Claus.

It was about 11:30 p.m. when I pulled into the driveway on Arch Street. Momsy was waiting for us. She just glared. "I brought him home," I said, "Just like you asked." I climbed the stairs and went to bed. I think Willie passed out the moment he hit the mattress in the downstairs bedroom. Momsy, the next day, said nothing to me about the incident. I think she was torn between disgust and gratitude. I'll never know. I am not proud of that night. I included the story because I think it says something about the three of us. I have never drunk whiskey since.

Roger went on from high school in 1962 to work as a brakeman for the Erie-Lackawanna Railroad (we jokingly called it the Erie-Lackamoney) for 18 years; then was a plumber at Allegheny College for 24 years. In retirement, he worked very hard to serve his church and became assistant to the minister of First Christian Church in Meadville. He eventually obtained a diploma from Liberty University on his own and the church ordained him. He currently is associate minister there.

The early bowling lessons paid off. Roger was a professional bowler in the regional circuit for two years and in the senior national circuit for one year. He can boast of seven perfect games. Several years ago he was inducted into the Western Crawford County Bowling Hall of Fame and is listed in the International Bowling Hall of Fame.

Momsy was an eternal optimist. She greeted everyone with a warm smile, even during tough times, and loved to laugh. She never complained about the life she had been given. She rarely cried.

136

The day of the fire, she did. And tears came when a friend or relative died. The time she cried that I remember best was in 1961. She had driven me to the train station in the early morning to see me off to Cleveland, where I would be inducted for my three-year enlistment in the Army. Don was working at the Pittsburgh YMCA and was soon to go to Marine Corps officer training school. Art had enlisted in the Army the year before and was in Monterey, California, at language school. Momsy was saying goodbye for a long time to her last Thompson child at home. She stood on the platform and I could see tears running down her cheeks as I watched from the moving train. I shed a few, too.

When she retired from the courthouse, Momsy spent a great deal of time with her grandchildren – including my children in a time of great personal need. She gave tons of care to Art's son, Colin (1967-1997), who lived his life afflicted by cerebral palsy. Then she finished her caregiver years as a volunteer "grandmother" for residents at Polk Center.

When she sold the Arch Street house, Art drove Momsy around Meadville to pay all of the remaining debts from those 30 years. He said beneficiaries, such as those who had run the Hilgendorf Dairy out on Route 19, were more than a little surprised to see an old written-off account settled out of the blue. Momsy had two more overriding goals in life. One was that all of her children would obtain college degrees. We all did except Miriam, who left school because of her family obligations, but she certainly earned the equivalent as time went by. The other was that her

children would all outlive her. That came to be.
Momsy died in 1983, well-loved and debt-free.

First-class MASH's first class

The new Meadville Area Senior High School at the east end of North Street opened in the fall of 1958. It was nicknamed MASH long before the TV series about the Korean War Army field hospital. The old high school had been called just Meadville High School. The new school was first class and we were the first class of seniors.

The brightness and airiness of the new school was in sharp contrast to the dark, dungeon-like interior of the old high school. Everything was brand new. You had to be enthusiastic and excited. That is, unless you were always tired, as I was.

My work pace couldn't be sustained without cost. It began to tell on my health and ability to keep up with the growing challenges at school. In the fall, I cut my work hours and went out for football. But after a week or two of practice, I met with Rudy Gradisek, the coach I had known for years, and told him I was pushing things too hard. He told me he was from an immigrant family and knew all too well why it was necessary for some high schoolers to opt for work. "Some things are more important than football," he said. I quit the team with a sense of dignity, though I knew he really wanted me to play.

John Joy, the legendary basketball coach, stopped me in the hall when I came back from Slippery Rock and asked me why I had not come out for the team. I told him I had to go to work. It turned out to be a very good team without me. It was rare for Coach Joy to ask someone to try out for the team. Everyone wanted to play for him.

In my senior year I was absent 30 days of that 180-day school year, though I was never ill, just tired. Most weeks I was working from 2 a.m. to 8 a.m.; then from 4 p.m. to 10 p.m. at The Lamplighter. I don't remember when I slept at home. My advisor did not know what to do with me. As long as my grades remained high, it was a standoff.

As a junior, I asked to join the Debate Team. Miss Adelaide deMaison, the team advisor, not so subtly told me she didn't think I was right for the group and encouraged me to focus on sports. I don't think she knew who my father was. He once argued a case before the U.S. Supreme Court, quite a feat for a small-town lawyer. It was mentioned in his obituary.

In the fall of 1957, after the Soviet Union launched that tiny spacecraft named Sputnik I, President Dwight D. Eisenhower called for a national crash program to develop scientists. Great emphasis was suddenly placed on math and science in Meadville schools. I rebelled. I don't know why. But I was coming to realize that history is the most important subject, and reading is the best way to learn history. I still believe that today. I dropped out of Joe Wursek's physics class. He took me aside and said he was upset. "You are one of the students who actually understand physics," he said. It was an extra course on my junior year schedule. I was flattered by what he said, but dropped the course anyway.

In my senior year at MASH, I opted for the easier of two math classes. It was taught by Donald "Speedball" Cropp. I can't remember whether it was trigonometry, or solid geometry, or a combination, or something else. I wasn't too interested. I finally made a deal with Mr. Cropp that I would sit at the back of the classroom and study English. In return, I would listen enough to be sure to pass all of the math tests and I agreed to refrain from playing any tricks on him.

I had Mrs. Margaret Bradley for English that year. It followed math, so I had a good chance to go in with my homework fresh in my mind. We had one really big book report to present to the class. Mrs. Bradley encouraged us to choose from the classics. Instead, I chose the contemporary novel, "Peyton Place" by Grace Metalious. After all, it is very well-written; is about high school seniors in a small town, as we were; and deals with real-life issues. It was on *The New York Times* Best Seller List for 59 weeks after its release in 1956. I went to the 1957 film version five times down at the Academy Theatre. The fifth time, I closed my eyes and just listened to the music. But the novel includes some vivid sex scenes and some pretty bad behavior by some adults. Mrs. Bradley did not think it appropriate. It was the best book report I ever gave, save maybe that on Hitler's "Mein Kampf" in history class the year before. Mrs. Bradley gave me a "C." I learned then there is no accounting for taste.

I would doze off a lot at my desk that year. In the 1959 Yearbook, classmate Bill Smith wrote: "… Please don't sleep through your college classes." When I was teaching a class at Allegheny in 2002, one of my students kept falling asleep in class. It was very frustrating. I realized only then how my teachers back at MASH might have felt about me when they had to wake me up.

I did get another taste of culture during high school. The Latin Club in the spring of 1958 put on a play. Most of the members were in the Class of 1960. I had never seen a dancer perform before, save for a couple of square dances out at the East Mead Fire Hall. Judy Maitland, already an accomplished ballerina, performed for the play. I was taken by how graceful she was. It gave me a new appreciation for the fine arts.

I had long before memorized the English language version of Marc Antony's funeral oration from Shakespeare's "Julius Caesar." I secretly hoped I would be chosen to present it in the play. But I was competing with Glenn Hickernell. He was a natural actor and did a fine job. I was given a part, however. It was to play the shroud-draped corpse of Julius Caesar himself, laid out on a slab that normally was a cafeteria table. I managed to get through it without flinching or interrupting Glenn. Both Judy and Glenn later were accomplished pros in their respective fields.

I did manage some involvement in school activities those final two years. Besides Latin Club, I was a member of the Scholastic Honor Society and the International Relations Club. And I was president of the History Club. I played volleyball because there was little practice time needed and it earned me a coveted varsity letter. I never could afford the jacket to put it on, though. The History Club presidency was quite a coup as I was competing with David Bates, Dr. Richard Bates' son, who very much wanted the position. My secret weapons were club members Bob Say, Bob Buttermore and Max Maloney Jr., who quietly lined up votes for me. They playfully called me "Der Führer." We had some fun in that group. In the 1959 yearbook History Club photo, classmates can see me posing beside David in my ink-stained shirt. He was wearing a suit and tie. I'm not proud of that comparison. It is just the way it was. David and I later became good friends and we remained so until his death a few years ago.

One of my absences that year was during the 1959 flood. Rescuers were using a rope line to hoist people from the flooded Fifth Ward across French Creek to safety on the east bank. I had to see it. The rescue was dramatic. We bystanders were relieved that no one fell into the raging waters. My cousin Bill Brink worked at his brother's service station at the new South Park Avenue Plaza, across Smock Bridge from the city. When the flood waters surged in, Bill lifted himself on the hydraulic car rack and sat out the flood near the roof of the building. He later told us he swam to safety, but if I know Bill, he probably waded to safety when the waters receded. As a reporter a few years later, I wrote about construction of the Army Corps of Engineers Union City Dam upstream in Erie County. It and the Woodcock Creek Dam finally tamed French Creek. Meadville has experienced no such flooding since.

Henry Abbiw, our exchange student from Ghana, West Africa, and I almost made news the next year. We both had started at Allegheny and I decided that Henry should see a big league baseball game. We drove to Cleveland in my 1952 Plymouth with one or two friends. He enjoyed the game and thought the name Indians for the home team was not insulting to Native Americans. But what happened next was insulting to Henry. We stopped on Euclid Avenue for a sundae at a well-known, upscale ice cream shop. We stood in the doorway waiting to be seated, but no one responded. Finally, I asked for a table and a waiter indicated in pretty strong words that blacks were not welcome there. I usually don't get upset, but I

143

asked for the manager and told him we had an exchange student from Africa who wanted an American ice cream sundae and we intended to get it. They seated us in the rear of the restaurant and we – eventually – were served. Henry and I never dreamed we would become a small part of the Civil Rights movement. No reporters showed up, however, and the incident was lost to history. Incidentally, we had no Dairy Queens or McDonald's back then. Ice cream stands were scarce and usually family-owned.

Remember my playmate Tom Henderson? I saw him once more. It was one of those chance meetings in a far-off place. It was in 1964 and I was at an Army communications post on an old Luftwaffe air base in southern Germany. Attached to the post was a missile detachment. It was only a week or two before my return to the States on a troop ship and my discharge from active duty. I was walking near the PX (Post Exchange) and saw three African-Americans approaching. They were from the missile detachment. One of them was Tom. I stopped them and asked, "Are you Tom Henderson?" "Yes," he said. "I'm your old buddy from Meadville, Jim Thompson," I said. "We used to play together all the time."

Tom gave me a rather cold acknowledgement. I suggested we get together before my departure and chat about old times. He said he would call me, but with little enthusiasm. I told him my barracks phone number. No call came. That was it. I think the message I got from this encounter was the difference in the racial divide between an urban mixed-race community such as Aliquippa, a suburb of Pittsburgh, and a small city such as Meadville. I believe Tom had to take on a different demeanor when his family moved to the big city. I don't blame him. It is the way it was, and often, still is. Had I met him when he was walking alone, I think the outcome would have been different.

'Forgiven'

As high school graduation approached in the spring of 1959, I was eager to get on to college. I was not proud of the absences and it was not until the next year as a freshman at Allegheny that I realized how ill-prepared I was for college. A lot of my knowledge gap could have been overcome had I achieved perfect attendance during my senior year and studied harder. I took a hiatus from Allegheny after two years, both to answer President John F. Kennedy's call to serve my country and to find a way to better prepare for serious study in English literature and history. At his inauguration in January 1961, the youthful JFK challenged us with the words: "Ask not what your country can do for you; ask what you can do for your country." Art had enlisted in the U.S. Army Security Agency after high school in 1960. I decided to do the same a year later, with a three-year enlistment. I left Allegheny on good terms. My advisor at that time, Dr. Pommer, helped me prepare a 100-book reading list, which I completed during 18 months in Turkey and a year in Germany. I finally became a serious student when I returned to Allegheny in 1965.

I felt JFK's inaugural address probably was the most stirring speech in America since Lincoln's Gettysburg Address. But an equally important speech, I believe now, was President Dwight D. Eisenhower's farewell address, also in 1961. In it, the great general and world leader warned Americans of the potential dangers of the huge military-industrial complex that had been created to enable us to win World War II. It could become too powerful, he said. I think it has.

I had to work on prom night, but did manage to show up for graduation. The teachers were all present. Stewart Hoffman had gotten over my refusal to take his tough math class. Joe Wursek was dividing his time between his physics classes and his drive-in restaurant business in Saegertown. Mrs. Bradley and Miss deMaison would both have collapsed in dead faints if some muse had told them I would end up an English major. Donald Cropp heaved a sigh of relief that I was leaving his classroom for good. The attendance and counseling offices likely shredded my records.

Social Studies guru Donald Leberman and I had a warm relationship. I loved his Problems of Democracy class. But it was too much for him when I showed up for graduation wearing my new white bucks – the hottest footwear since Elvis immortalized blue suede shoes. The graduation gown covered my worn checkered shirt and jeans as we waited off-stage. But the shoes were exposed and were too much for Mr. Leberman. Conformity was a big thing with most of our teachers and the administrators who ran the Meadville public schools. Mr. Leberman was always impeccably dressed. It was probably a good thing that some of us from time to time challenged the expected behavior. It sort of prepped all of us for what was to come in the 1960s. But this wasn't the time. Mr. Leberman took off his shiny black dress shoes and strongly encouraged me to switch. I made my way across the stage in sort of a victory shuffle in ill-fitting shoes. But I also credited Mr. Leberman for responding effectively to an unexpected crisis.

The amazing thing about those 311 students who walked across the stage that day is their collective record of achievement. Among our classmates are doctors, scientists, lawyers, educators, journalists, industrial and business leaders, craftsmen, social workers, artists, family makers, and more. I think we can match any other public high school in America.

High school had one more ritual. That was signing our yearbook, "The Bulldog," on the final day of school. As I was looking through my copy recently, one signature brought back the fondest memory. All through high school, I had played tricks on our very vulnerable librarian, Adelaide Courtney. She was a plain, quiet woman who had a very well-developed bosom. I nicknamed her "Bubbles," and often playfully addressed her that way. For some reason, I gravitated to the library whenever I could. I sometimes snoozed there, played jokes on the staff, or occasionally did some serious thinking or research. Miss Courtney tolerated my behavior because it was only mildly disruptive. She and I knew the boundaries. I was careful not to ruin a good thing.

On the last day of school I made my last trip to the library and asked her to sign my yearbook. She looked surprised. Under her photo in the faculty pages I had written, "Bubbles." She just smiled. Then, above the photo she wrote her name, Adelaide H. Courtney, in beautiful script. And above it, the word: "Forgiven." What a wonderful gesture! It was the highlight of my high school career.

PHYSICAL EDUCATION: John Joy, Vera Rummel, Kenneth Nelson.

LIBRARIAN: Adelaide Courtney.

"Bubbles"

ATHLETIC DEPART-
MENT: seated—Orie Cox, James DiMaria, John Joy, Louis Beltz; standing—Kenneth Nelson, Thomas Bullish, Arthur Lehman, Tom Duff.

'Forgiven': Adelaide H. Courtney.

Epilogue

My peers might wonder if I am writing this on some kind of ego trip. No. I have already noted that my childhood was not really that special, considering the post-war era and all of the economic and social upheavals taking place in our society. Nor was I ever a true scholar, a great athlete, nor acclaimed nationally in my profession – for which feats an autobiography or memoir is in demand.

I guess it is just that this is the place and time for me to do this. As a journalist, I wrote about other people for 36 years. I realize I am getting old. But I can still recall my childhood and type well on my ergonomic keyboard. Many of my old friends are still with us and can help fill in the blanks in my memory. Too many others are gone. I realize that Donald C. Thompson's old log book is our family's most valuable possession. I am so happy that he took the time to keep it. It gives me the opportunity to explore his life, and to gain an understanding of the society in which he lived. Other discoveries in my genealogy research the past several years have been a book written about the Thompsons and the Boylans, titled: "Frontier Farmer: Autobiography and Family History of Aaron A. Boylan," edited by Katherine Lytle Sharp. A Boylan married a Thompson in the early days of Union City and the book gives the reader a wonderful picture of pioneer life in western Pennsylvania. Also of great personal value are two books about Bishop Roberts and his family – Tippy's and one by the Rev. Charles Elliott, which describes the 1798 trek to Shenango. These books have enriched my life greatly. So, I want to do my part and leave something, too. For whom I leave it does not really matter. Perhaps the family will produce another history buff somewhere down the road.

Readers likely will see this work as a memoir; an autobiography if you will. Some also will see in it an historical account of a middle-American city in the middle of the past century. Some will see in it the experiences and hopes of the Class of 1959. But I realized only as I was reviewing the final document that what I had written is more than these. It is an odyssey – the never-ending search by a boy for the father he never knew. In these pages, I think I have come as close as I ever will to finding him.

My companion, Alice Moomy, and I were sitting at the bar at our Elks lodge for our customary afternoon social gathering with fellow retirees when the odyssey aspect of the book struck me. Lodge member Victoria Allen was sitting nearby. She asked how the book was coming along and wanted to know a little more about it. I said without thinking, "It's a boy's search for the father he never knew." When I said that, I started to cry. Yes, grown men do cry sometimes. It took me a minute or two to stop the tears and go on with the conversation around the bar. It certainly was an emotional moment for me.

Looking back over the journey, I can't help but think about the importance of timing in one's life. Had we the medicines I take now, my father's diabetes probably would have been manageable and he would have lived another 10 to 20 years. If we had the know-how in the 1950s to treat blemished skin by zapping the oil glands in the cheeks, I would not have become the poster boy for acne creams and suffered the angst that went with it. Or, had we all been born a few years later, we might have had a long class casualty list from the Vietnam War. Twenty years earlier, and some would have been World War II casualties.

I'd say our timing, overall, was pretty good. It was a great childhood – even for a ragtag mid-America street urchin.

-finis-

Class reunion, June 2014; urchin is below ..ass in Class.
(Author's note: humor intended)

About the author: James Emory Thompson is a 1969 graduate of Allegheny College. He enlisted in the U.S. Army Security Agency from 1961 to 1964, serving in Turkey and Germany. He was a reporter for *The Meadville Tribune* from 1965 to 1968. He then joined the *Erie Daily Times* and *Sunday Times-News* for a career that covered 33 years. He held numerous newsroom posts, but primarily was a government and courthouse reporter, columnist and political writer. He served on the Times Publishing Company Editorial Board for 25 of those years. Mr. Thompson has done graduate work at Gannon and Edinboro universities, and has taught classes at Allegheny and Villa Maria colleges and Edinboro University of Pennsylvania. He has two daughters and four grandchildren and resides with his companion, Alice Moomy, in Millcreek Township, Erie County. This work is based on Mr. Thompson's remembrances of childhood and conversations with classmates over the years. It is intended to be factual. Any errors or slights are his responsibility, and he hopes no one will be offended. He expresses his deep gratitude for the dozen or so relatives and classmates who helped fill in so many blanks. They know who they are. Ten who must be mentioned by name are classmate Eric Johnson; classmate Ed Hines; Art and Judy Thompson; the Rev. Roger C. Smith; classmates and my four best boosters, Bob Say, Chuck Anderson, Bob Waid and Ed Morfenski; and classmate Saundra Gourley, who generously sent me her 1956 edition of the "Bulldog" to help in the research. And a special thanks to Alice for patiently giving me the time I needed to undertake this project in the midst of our already-busy schedule. Visit the author at www.mid-americastreeturchin.com.

James Emory Thompson, 2013, Ernest Hemingway pose.

What classmates are saying:

What an incredible gift by Jim! It was a real page turner and I couldn't put it down. My father, a gifted engineer, died when I was 11. Some of your (Jim's) growing up experiences mirrored mine. I had a job when I was 13 and worked as a soda jerk at Big Wirts; then as a stock market girl at Kay Richards where I had to wear nylons and started a school rage that canned bobbysocks. That work lasted until the end of my first year at Allegheny, where I ate a hamburger and walked down the "Hill" to my afternoon job, which I loved. I love

well-written books with historical notes such as Jim wrote.
–Lynn Atwell

Just finished your book and found it very informative as well as a trip down memory lane. Will never forget JET, DOT and ART. As I read, I had to stop and wipe my eyes from time to time. One never knows of the hardships incurred by friends especially in our childhood. ... Laddie was a great dog and when you saw Laddie, somewhere near was Miriam. Your mother was very kind and extremely tolerant of the stuff we did in our back yards. ... Really, Really enjoyed your book. ...
–Don Riddle

Enjoyed reading my sister's (Carol Schroeder Prather) copy of the book about the old catcher for Coke. Remember the Triumph when we were hit from behind when you took me to watch a basketball game at Farrell. Thanks for the kind words about my family. ... Thanks again, really enjoyed the book.
–George Schroeder

Just a short note to thank you so much for including me in sending Jim's book. I started this morning and, my! I can hardly stop! ...
–Yvonne Mulder '60

I have read the book; actually I could not put it down. Jim, it is quite an amazing account of you, your family, your town, high school, the whole works. It was fascinating and so interesting and enjoyable. ...
–Bob Bates Jr.

Here's my brother's e mail. He loved your book as I did. Thank you for writing it and sharing with us (Sandy Zduniak). My name is Ron Truran, a big brother of Sandy Truran, a classmate of yours in the Class of 1959. She was kind enough to send me your book ... and while reading every word, in some ways I relived part of my Meadville life. First District School, MHS, etc. ... God Bless you for your story, and my opportunity to read it.
–Ron Truran

Thanks for writing your memories of growing up in Meadville. You don't
know how much I appreciated reading familiar names, places and activities
growing up there, too. I graduated in the Class of 1958, left Meadville in 1960, have been back many times as I have relatives there. It will always be "home" to me with fond memories. I congratulate you on this accounting of life in the 1940s and 1950s. We grew up in the best of times, as far as I am concerned. Thank you so very much, Jim.
–Patty DeLoss O'Brien

Your "Urchin" certainly brims with facts that just amaze me! I don't know how you did it! And I pass my hearty congratulations on for a job well done! ...
–Tom Clark

I just finished reading Jim's book. I found it to be delightful and reminiscent of Mark Twain especially the story on the raft. He does a wonderful job of describing life in a small town during that period of time. ... There was certainly a lot of

humor in his book. I loved the story of the jeans with the holes. My grandson would pay $50 or more to buy jeans like that to be in style. Once I took him wearing those jeans to see my father who was in the hospital. When Corey left the room for a moment, my father scolded me and told me to buy that child some decent pants. I told Corey we should just buy some cheap jeans at a bargain store, put them on a fence post, shoot holes in them with a shotgun, run over them with a truck, and they would be exactly like what is in style. Jim did not know he was so stylish back in those days. ... and tell Jim that I commend him for overcoming such a rough start and having such a great finish! The book is great fun. Thanks again for sharing his book with me.
–Deanna Delozier Buttray

What a wonderful gift to our class! It was great working with Jim and the others in the bowels of the *Tribune* as a fellow inserter. We learned a lot about the work ethic; self-discipline in getting up and going to work at 2 a.m.; and about being a team player in getting the paper out. The experience served all of us well later in life.
–Ed Morfenski

I was able to download and read the entire book. It was very enjoyable and brought back my own personal memories of growing up in Meadville. Thanks for helping with the electronic version so all our class members can read it, too.
–Vito Valella

I was able to download the material and have enjoyed reading Jim's memoir. Hope he is able to get it published for the open book market.
–Ginny (Leberman) Pegelow

I was able to download Jim's manuscript and enjoyed it very much.
–Jim Rist

… Jim Thompson's book provides a relaxing trip down memory lane and reminds us that we've seen and experienced a lot. I hope and pray the future provides wonderful memories that we can comprehend and understand, because the world around us is moving at a pretty fast pace!
–Chuck Anderson

Written by MASH classmate Ed Hines
as a foreword to the June 2014 reunion edition
of "Adventures of a mid-America street urchin"

Jim Thompson has given his MASH Classmates a gift. More valuable than gold, it's a gift that is an emotional and detailed accounting of our past history in Meadville, Pennsylvania. It is a treasure and a keepsake. In these "Adventures of a mid-America street urchin," we see Jim and his two brothers and two sisters living what might be termed a prosperous life in a large home on the outskirts of Meadville. But, his attorney father passed away when Jim was two, and his Mother was left raising a family of five on very limited resources. By the end of the 1940s, Jim's Mother, to whom this autobiographical work is dedicated, had lost her husband, the hope for real estate in the estate settlement, and a medical doctor neighbor who could have provided health care. Then came the negative impact of post-War inflation.

Jim's story unfolds in a series of fascinating portraits of life in Meadville for an "urchin" of limited resources. There is the raft on a pond near French Creek, delivering the *Meadville Tribune* and the *Erie Daily Times,* cobbling together bicycle parts into something that could be ridden, a poem reciting at First District School, holey jeans, delivering advertising fliers for Straw's Grocery, adjusting to a stepfather and stepbrother, and the fire. Oh, the fire! This writer remembers being traumatized on his way to First District School that April 1, 1954, morning, seeing smoke pouring out of the windows of the Thompson House on North Main Street.

Jim showed us in graphic detail how important it was to have all of Meadville as his playground, including beautiful Shadybrook Park. He describes how an ethnic and religious multiplicity of friends provided a "melting pot" of experiences. A brush with petty theft, stealing Zagnut bars at Murphy's 5 & 10, provided a lesson, as did a boxing encounter with Meadville's police detective. We came to understand the importance of sports to this Meadville urchin and how organizations like Kiwanis and Ki-Y offer growth opportunities to young boys.

After a challenging family move to Slippery Rock, Jim returned to Meadville. He started in an entry food service job, rising to (the designation of) assistant to the chef. He continued work at the *Meadville Tribune*, where he had started with his brother as a bulk newspaper deliverer, requiring virtually an all-night presence.

One vital constant in Jim's life was his mother who, despite ill fortune and poverty, managed to keep the family together and encourage each boy or girl to find their own individuality and destiny. Her job at Allegheny College opened up an opportunity for Jim, with partial remission of tuition, to attend college after MASH graduation. After enrolling, Jim realized that patriotic service was calling, and he enlisted in the U.S. Army spending more than two years overseas. He returned to Allegheny in 1965, and completed college. A successful career in journalism followed in Meadville and Erie.

Jim's autobiography is important to his MASH classmates for at least three reasons. First, it provides an amazingly detailed, stereoscopic view of growing up in Meadville and environs during the

1940s, 1950s and 1960s. Each of us will relate to Meadville details in different ways, but the specificity and Jim's careful research paid dividends.

The second reason this autobiography is vital is that it shows how someone, finding himself suddenly in poverty, was able to draw on his considerable innate talents and do more than survive. He made the best of a situation that could have been fatal. He grew and developed into a productive human being against all odds. This autobiography provides numerous lessons to anyone finding themselves in a negative situation.

Finally, this autobiography demonstrates the critical importance of having social and medical services which are accessible to those in need, not as free handouts but targeted to those with demonstrated need. In today's competitive, isolationist environment, this is a valuable lesson. This writing gives us the rationale to foster community, organizational, and social service leaders who are trained and willing to provide role models for young people. It made all the difference to Jim Thompson, and it makes all the difference in a community's quality of life.

Ed Hines
Bloomington, Illinois

Made in the USA
Middletown, DE
09 May 2015